*One Year's Reading for Fun*

CECIL BEATON

*Bernard Berenson*

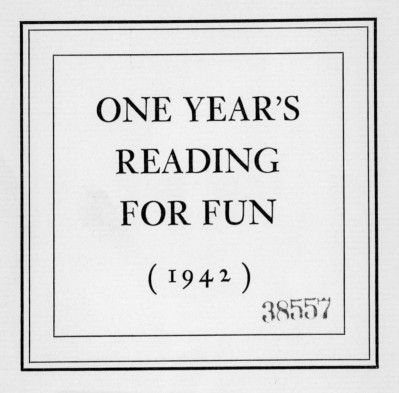

# ONE YEAR'S
# READING
# FOR FUN

( 1942 )

*Introduction by John Walker*

DIRECTOR OF THE NATIONAL GALLERY OF ART

*New York:* Alfred·A·Knopf

1 9 6 0

*The footnotes in this volume,*

*based in part on bibliographic data*

*assembled by Hannah Kiel,*

*have been prepared by*

*David Wolfe Biller*

L. C. catalog card number: 59–15316
© *Alfred A. Knopf, Inc.,* 1960

THIS IS A BORZOI BOOK,
PUBLISHED BY ALFRED A. KNOPF, INC.

FIRST EDITION

TO

*Judge Learned Hand*

WITH DEEP

AFFECTION

# Introduction

WHEN SIR THOMAS MORE was sent to the Tower, he recalled that he had always longed to be a monk but that, uncertain of his vocation, he had hesitated. Now the King had arranged that he should experience for the rest of his life the joys of a monastic solitude. In somewhat the same way, Bernard Berenson—or B. B., as he is known to his friends—found himself enjoying an enforced seclusion during the years in the last World War when it was not safe to be an American living in Italy. Those years, which B. B. says he looks back on with nostalgia, were in some respects the most creative of his life.

At the time America entered the war, approximately the date of the beginning of this diary, B. B. was seventy-seven years of age. His rise to a position of pre-eminence in the field of art history and criticism had begun in 1894, with the publication of his first book on Italian art. Among his earliest books, four on the principal schools of Renaissance painting in Italy offered a new aesthetic approach to pictures and have remained the best introduction to the study of Italian painting ever written. We, B. B.'s pupils, used to call them, jokingly and lovingly, the "Four Gospels." They were followed eventually by a book which listed, with attributions to individual artists, the significant pictures painted in Italy during the Renaissance. This volume we referred to as the "Book of Revelation." And it was on this that much of B. B.'s talent was dissipated. For the "revelations" were based on endless research and comparison and on the continual tracing of panels and canvases from one collection to another.

B. B. himself has said that he knows this was partly a waste of his energies, knows that he did not choose the most spiritually profitable pursuit, did not make the most of himself. True, his list of pictures and his definitive catalogue of Florentine drawings are of fundamental importance to us who work in museums. B. B., during those years of pure scholarship, mapped a continent of artistic achievement, gave us a basic guide where scientific charting was sorely needed. But, as the "Four Gospels" had proven, he was too great a genius to be a mere cartographer of art.

And then there was a second kind of waste, one for which B. B.'s friends were responsible. Throughout the diary the reader will note the fascination that Plato exerts on B. B. Is this fascination explained, perhaps, by Plato's having preserved conversation, his having passed on to us dialogues heard while walking with Socrates in the clear Attic sunlight? B. B.'s conversations with his friends as we roamed the Tuscan countryside, or sat in the loggia of "I Tatti," his villa near Florence, or as we warmed ourselves before the bright fire in his library—these dialogues, which we found so dazzlingly brilliant, all have vanished. For none of us was a Plato or even a Boswell.

But the war stopped both these kinds of waste. B. B. ceased to worry about the flotsam and jetsam of Italian paintings which formerly were constantly being brought to his attention; and, isolated from his friends, he wrote instead of talking. The result is a series of books, all composed during the war years, which are among the most stimulating and important published in our time. Of these recent writings, *A Year's Reading for Fun* offers in some ways the clearest picture of B. B. himself, of the scope of his interests, the fairness of his judgment, and the perceptiveness of his extraordinary intelligence.

With the war upon him, B. B. faced a terrifying future. In time of crisis some people go to church, some take to drink, others simply run away. B. B. turned to his library. The diary shows the remarkable degree to which, through absorption in reading, he managed to rise above the horror of current events. Surely, no one could have been in greater peril from Nazis and Fascists alike. B. B. was not only an American citizen; he was a Jew, and was well known as an anti-Fascist. Yet he declined the opportunity to be repatriated. He considered himself immobilized by the illness of his wife, Mary Berenson, and by the Italian nationality of his secretary, companion, and indispensable support, Nicky Mariano.

These three people, confronted by a catastrophe, resorted to what is, for one who can digest it, the most potent of all tranquilizers. They drugged themselves with reading. They had at hand one of the greatest private libraries ever assembled, and they had the advantage of extraordinary fluency in several languages. They read to themselves; they read to each other; they devoured book after book. And B. B. wrote down the ideas generated by this voracious absorption of the printed page.

His comments have a spontaneity that makes them seem almost like conversations between friends, about a book just laid aside. Desultory reading was always a favorite pastime at "I Tatti." How the diary recalls the sound of voices reading aloud—Nicky's lovely polyglot accent, each word so clearly enunciated, and yet a marvelous speed maintained; and Mary's slight lisp and Oxford pronunciation so carefully cultivated over the years that nothing of

Philadelphia remained—and then, when the reading has stopped, B. B.'s beautifully modulated voice commenting on what he has listened to.

B. B. has always seemed to me the perfect audience for an author: a reader passionately eager to get at the substance of a book and, if this eludes him, blaming himself for his lack of discernment. In the diary his interest is concentrated on each book's contribution to the enrichment of his own mind and to the satisfaction of his curiosity. When he has got to the heart of the writer's thesis, he analyzes it by his own standards; for his daily journal was not intended for publication, but rather as a container for the essences extracted from the books he was devouring.

I am amazed at the impartiality and objectivity of his judgments. Much as he loathes Hitler, for example, he points out the astuteness running through *Mein Kampf;* and, much as he loves Plato, he criticizes Socrates for his tendency to turn conversation into chess-play dialectics. He calls Churchill's *Marlborough* the most expensive book ever written, since if instead of taking the time to write it the author had exercised political power, he might have re-armed England and so have prevented the war. He admits that German metaphysics baffles him, yet he cannot resist, as he says, nibbling away at it. So much of his life has been spent in reading art historians that he now turns, for books on art, to writers with poetic insight. He reads especially Ruskin and Pater, and his comments on these writers are among the most interesting in the book.

As we follow through the pages, there gradually emerges a remarkable portrait of B. B. It is not so sharply focused as the one in *Sketch for a Self-Portrait;* rather, it is like a painting by Vuillard, the figure fusing with the background, here a library.

It is a fascinating image one glimpses, a human being of

*Introduction*

immense culture caught in a "manquake," as B. B. calls it, an irrational upheaval of passionate hatred. By reading he tries to find the explanation, the causes of this tragedy: he searches among the German Romantics for the genesis of modern Germany; he studies the personalities involved in the Treaty of Versailles for the more immediate causes; he turns to Herodotus for the effect of chance on history. His library is his fortress, and it is filled with the smoke of the battle raging outside.

History, philosophy, literature must yield up the explanation of this ghastly situation. B. B. turns to his books in this crisis with the same insatiable curiosity, the same confidence in a personal revelation that he has always brought to his study of the visual arts. This freshness of approach, unprejudiced by the opinions of others, gives B. B.'s diary its extraordinary vitality, just as a similar freshness of vision and indifference to authority have made him the greatest expert the world has known in his chosen field, to which, incidentally, he scarcely refers.

JOHN WALKER

JULY, 1959

# Author's Foreword

1942 was the first year in which I lived the quiet life of an alien enemy, cut off not only from my friends abroad but from my Italian friends as well and from the foreign press. Thanks to the promise given by Ciano to our ambassador, William Phillips, I was not molested in any way and had ideal leisure for reading or for being read to. I confess that I look back to that time with a certain nostalgia. So contradictory is human nature!

Some readers may find my notes a bit short, abrupt, sometimes almost cryptic. They must remember that at the time I wrote them I had no other idea than to try to put into words what was flitting through my mind and to stop myself from thinking too much of the war and all its consequences. I have left what I wrote in 1942 unaltered, even if in several instances I do not entirely take the same view today that I did then.

There is only one point I want to elucidate. The word "Greek" and the name of Plato occur so often that I run the risk of being taken for a Greek philologist or for a Platonic metaphysician. I am neither. Ever since my boyhood I have enjoyed Greek as a language and as literature. I was able to read it with fair facility. Now I am reduced to the use of crutches in the shape of the Loeb or Busé editions with the translation on the opposite page. As for Plato, I have reveled and still revel in his ironical and satirical fun at the expense of the sophists of his day and even more in his straightforward account of the symposium and of the death of Socrates.

In connection with Plato I want to add a curious bit of information to what I said about his *Critias* (see July 29th). It comes to me from my recent reading and is of particular interest to us Americans.

Plato had probably little if any visual notion in his head when he wrote about the capital city of his Atlantis, but in the middle of the eighteenth century a French architect, Ledoux, published an attempt of reducing it to visual terms. On this plan the important buildings are in the center from which the great avenues run out like the spokes of a wheel and are in their turn pierced by concentric streets. The avenues are for the authorities and the administration, the streets for the ordinary citizen. It never occurred to me, I am ashamed to confess, that the city of Washington in the District of Columbia is the realization of this Platonic ideal.

After the thirteen colonies decided to federalize into one nation, they set aside a certain territory made up of bits taken from two of the new states and called it the District of Columbia. Pierre L'Enfant, a French-born architect who had been a pupil and follower of Ledoux, was asked by George Washington to draw the plans for the capital city. And thus it remains to this day.

B. B.

Casa al Dono
August, 1958

*One Year's Reading for Fun*

# January 1942

| S | M | T | W | T | F | S |
|---|---|---|---|---|---|---|
|   |   |   |   | 1 | 2 | 3 |
| 4 | 5 | 6 | 7 | 8 | 9 | 10 |
| 11 | 12 | 13 | 14 | 15 | 16 | 17 |
| 18/25 | 19/26 | 20/27 | 21/28 | 22/29 | 23/30 | 24/31 |

1 JANUARY Between tea and dinner yesterday glanced at *Osservatore Romano, Deutsche Allgemeine Zeitung,* and *Wir und Italien.* In *Byzantinische Zeitschrift,* a long review of Stroub's *Vom Herrscherideal in der Spätantike,* by Treitinger, and of the latter's *Die oströmische Kaiser- und Reichsidee,* by Ostrogorsky. After dinner Mary [Mrs. Berenson] aloud, in Ranke's *Popes,* account of Jansenism, admirable.[1] Then Nicky [Mariano] aloud, Tarlé in his *Napoléon,* clear and succinct account of how Continental Blockade worked.[2] Last, Calamandrei's story of his childhood.[3]

[1] *The History of the Popes: Their Church and Their State* (3 vols., London, 1840, 1931) was written by Leopold von Ranke (1795–1896), the German historian who has been called the father of the modern objective school of historical writing.

[2] Eugène Tarlé (1874–    ) began his teaching career at St. Petersburg in 1899. He has been a leader in the newer Soviet historical school, which has substituted a nationalistic or patriotic trend for the earlier class-struggle emphasis. His *Napoléon* (Paris, 1937) is a French translation from the original Russian edition of 1927.

[3] *Inventario della Casa di Compagna* (Florence, 1945; first edition privately printed, 1941). Piero Calamandrei (1889–1956), an emi-

3

2 JANUARY By myself, yesterday a.m., Suarez's *Briand*, Volume V, grotesque portrait of Curzon and D'Abernon,[4] and today, Briand on thorny question of reparations. Confirms growing conviction that the fundamental mistake of the Versailles Peace was its not being based on the German certainty that they had been worsted in battle. We should have marched to Berlin, or even to Königsberg, and made the treaty there, occupying the country till fulfillment seriously started. ⁓ Then five pages of Herodotus, Book VIII, story of Clisthenes and his daughter's suitors, also end of Miltiades. Today, the strange story of Lemnian Pelasgians raping Athenian women. Wonder what is behind it.[5]

3 JANUARY After dinner yesterday, Nicky aloud, Odoacer and Theodoric in Amédée Thierry's *Récits d'histoire romaine.*[6] By myself Volkelt, *Das Tragische.*[7] ⁓ To-

---

nent Italian jurist, was an opponent of the Mussolini regime. In 1945 he founded the literary magazine *Il Ponte.*

[4] Georges Suarez (1890–1944): *Briand: Sa Vie, son Œuvre avec son Journal* (5 vols., Paris, 1938–41). The period covered at this point in B. B.'s reading is that of the series of international conferences following World War I, during which Lord Curzon was Britain's Foreign Secretary and Edgar Vincent D'Abernon (later Baron of Esher) was the British ambassador to Germany.

[5] B. B. at this time was well along on his third reading, over the years, of Herodotus' *History of the Persian Wars* in the original Greek. The edition he used was that of the Loeb Classical Library (4 vols., 1921), with A. D. Godley's English translation facing the Greek text page by page.

[6] *Récits de l'histoire romaine au V° siècle* (Paris, 1860) is the work of Simon-Dominique-Amédée Thierry (1797–1873), the younger brother of the more noted historian Augustin Thierry. Amédée Thierry wrote other studies of Roman history and biographies of religious figures; he was also active in the politics of his time.

[7] Johannes Volkelt (1848–1930): *Aesthetik des Tragischen* (Munich, 1896, 1923). B. B. wrote elsewhere later that Volkelt, of whom he was completely unaware until 1941, had apparently arrived independently at much the same theory of art-enjoyment as his

day, in Herodotus, of Xerxes' preparation to invade Greece, and of discussions in counsel of hotheaded Mardonius and wise old Artabanus, and of a huge, handsome presence haunting Xerxes after appearing to him again and again commanding him not to oppose destiny. I recall that according to Herodotus, Mycerinus incurred the wrath of the gods by opposing himself to destiny. ⁓ Tarlé on beginning of Napoleon's campaign in Russia. ⁓ Radio: Bach, Schumann, Pizzetti, Wagner. The last abominably rendered.

4 JANUARY Glanced as usual at Vatican sacristy sheet known as *Osservatore Romano*, and at *Deutsche Allgemeine*. Mary read aloud political articles in November *Atlantic*—the last we shall see for the "duration." Mary again after dinner, Ranke on papacy at turn of the eighteenth century. ⁓ Nicky, more Tarlé, still Russian campaign. ⁓ By myself many pages of Suarez's *Briand*, about Briand's visit to Washington. French seem incapable of understanding anything Anglo-Saxon. Nothing more remote from what I know of A. J. Balfour or [Charles Evans] Hughes than Suarez's attempt to characterize them.

5 JANUARY In Herodotus, Xerxes reaches the height of anthropomorphizing in lashing, fettering, and branding the Hellespont for disobeying him. The one thing no Persian king could stand was being asked release from military service. Xerxes has just been praising the Lydian Pythius for his more than princely generosity toward him and his army, but when this same Pythius begs that his eldest son be released, as he is sending four others, Xerxes immediately has the

---

own—fully stated in the essays *The Florentine Painters* (1896) and *The Central Italian Painters* (1897)—and had perhaps even anticipated him.

young man cut in half. ⁓ In Suarez, Briand's visit to Washington and misunderstandings. How avoidable, seeing he had Rosé as interpreter. There the English have a great advantage in U.S.A.

6 JANUARY Impressed by discussion between Artabanus and his nephew Xerxes, the first tragic-minded, the second sentimental and violent but not stupid. Artabanus goes on being skeptical about the outcome of the expedition against Athens, despite the brave show made by the invading forces. He says land and sea are the worst enemies, to which Xerxes replies that if one stopped to think of all that might befall, one would never undertake anything. True, for every serious train of heartless clear thinking leads to *zero*.

7 JANUARY Finished Volume 5 of Suarez's *Briand*, ending with account of Cannes meeting. Confirms all I thought at moment of Poincaré and even of Millerand, both worse than I thought, blind to facts and "human, too human" in their envy, jealousy, and spite.[8] As the book goes on, Suarez forgets to sneer and rage against the British, although at the Washington conference he finds fault grotesquely with Balfour. ⁓ Nicky read aloud Pirenne's *Mohammed and Charlemagne*.[9] Begins with best short account

[8] Aristide Briand's liberalism and advocacy of international organization exposed him to attack throughout his eleven terms as Premier of France. In 1920, Alexandre Millerand, by then an ardent nationalist, became President. It was during his tenure that Briand was replaced by former President Raymond Poincaré, an inflexible advocate of harsh reparations from Germany.

[9] Henri Pirenne (1862–1935), Belgian historian, traced the traditional and economic forces at work in medieval history. According to him, the unity and continuity of the ancient and medieval worlds remained unshaken until the Arab invasion. *Mahomet et Charlemagne*, published posthumously in Paris in 1937, has ap-

6

yet of Roman world, particularly of France in fifth and sixth centuries. ∼ By myself article by Einaudi on free trade, etc.[1] No wonder *Argomenti* has been suppressed where it appears.

8 JANUARY Mary read aloud yesterday evening, finishing Ranke's *Popes*. Disappointed not to find there story of Jesuits in Paraguay, whom I vividly recall as being there. ∼ Tarlé's account of Napoleon in Russia, how he might have saved himself by proclaiming emancipation of serfs, but was too bourgeois to do so, and besides feared it might result in his finding nobody to treat of peace, if Alexander and his system perished. I don't see that it could have resulted in more than seriously threatening the Tsar but yet leaving him to rule and make peace.

9 JANUARY In Ruskin's letters to Norton,[2] his obdurate fury against the North for fighting against the South in our Civil War. He could not and would not think. It is

---

peared in English as *Mohammed and Charlemagne* (New York, 1939, 1955).

[1] Luigi Einaudi (1874–    ), a noted economist, was a member of the Italian senate after 1919 and opposed Fascism as early as 1924. After the war, he became Italy's first constitutional President (1948–55).

[2] *Letters of John Ruskin to Charles Eliot Norton, 1855–87* (2 vols., Boston, 1905). The letters begin after Ruskin (1819–1900) had already published the works on which was based his reputation as "art dictator" and defender of Pre-Raphaelite painting and architecture. The correspondence encompasses the period of his break with organized religion and with the British upper class, of his intense interest in political economy, of his later influential career as England's first professor of art, and finally, of his physical and mental collapse. Norton (1827–1908) was an editor of the *North American Review* before serving (1875–98) as professor of the history of art at Harvard. He also translated Dante—in fact, B. B.'s first experience of *The Divine Comedy* was with Norton at Harvard in 1885—and edited John Donne's works and letters of Carlyle, Emerson, Lowell, and Ruskin.

obvious that the South would have insisted on getting a slice of territory which the North could not have consented to. ⁓ Reread after nearly fifty years the martyrdom of Fra Michele Minorita, burnt in Florence toward end of fourteenth century for insisting that Pope John II was a heretic for denying that Christ and His Apostles owned any individual or communal property.[3] Interesting how much the Florentines have remained unchanged. They would behave the same today (except, as then, the very few) toward anyone willing to die for his faith.

10 JANUARY Further in Ruskin's to Norton: his misery, his savage bitterness over the disintegration following the loss of his brand of Christianity. ⁓ Began, Mary aloud, Winston Churchill's life of Marlborough, which promises entertainment.[4] ⁓ Began by myself Shirer's *Berlin Diary*,[5] sickening me with reminders of how much I felt, when it happened, of what he described. ⁓ Nicky aloud Tieck's *Ein Dichterleben*—garrulous, *à la* Heinse, but with charming touches and a discreetly romantic account of the young Shakespeare as seen through Marlowe's eyes.[6]

[3] *"Storia di Fra Michele Minorita come fu arso in Firenze nel 1389,"* in Zambrini: *Curiosita Letterarie del Secolo XIII al XVII* (Bologna, 1864).

[4] *Malborough: His Life and Times* (4 vols., London, 1933–38). John Churchill (1650–1722), the English general and statesman, became the first Duke of Marlborough in 1702. Sir Winston's special interest in Marlborough is obvious: his own grandfather was the seventh Duke.

[5] William L. Shirer (1904–   ): *Berlin Diary: The Journal of a Foreign Correspondent* (New York, 1941). The period covered is the explosive one from 1934 to 1941.

[6] Ludwig von Tieck (1773–1853)—dramatist, poet, novelist—was a leading figure in the German romantic movement, which owes much to his criticism and satire. Shakespeare was one of his great enthusiasms: in addition to his study in *Ein Dichterleben* (1826–31), he collaborated on the standard German translations of the plays.

8

11 JANUARY Pirenne's *Charlemagne et Mahomet* or, rather, the other way around, begins with the best account of material civilization in the sixth century that I have yet encountered, although of course it had no single fact to tell me that I did not really know. But to recall anything I must read about it again, and again, and again. ~ *Berlin Diary* most distressing. To me chiefly interesting on account of the crowd's reaction to everything, e.g., nobody seeing anything reprehensible in the invasion of Poland. It was the same here and, I suspect, the same everywhere on the Continent.

12 JANUARY More Herodotus. What a sinister humbug the Delphian oracle, and how could Greeks tolerate its immense power. ~ More *Berlin Diary*, heartbreaking account of German callousness to suffering inflicted on other people, and Allied incompetence. ~ In letters to Norton, Ruskin rages against Stuart Mill and economists in general. His premises are right, but how difficult for others to accept at his time!

13 JANUARY Pirenne gets even more satisfactory until he talks about art. There he follows [Louis] Bréhier and goes wrong with him, although once and again protesting. ~ More of Churchill's *Marlborough*, whole story of M.'s courtship and marriage, ending with an exaggerated attack on Macaulay, although he nearly realizes that Macaulay meant no harm, but needed a villain for his drama, just as gossips need something savory when talking about somebody whom as a matter of fact they like and admire and in their heart know to be innocent.

14 JANUARY Volume of Edna St. Vincent Millay's verses,[7] got little out of them. ~ Began correspondence of

[7] *The Harp-Weaver and Other Poems,* 1923.

9

Stefan George with Hofmannsthal, the latter only seventeen, the first six years older. Something sinister must have happened almost at once, for H. refused to see S. G. again, had his own father interfere, and continued being shy of meeting him, although ready enough to keep up a literary connection.[8] Surprised at H.'s precocity. At eighteen he was an accomplished versifier and confesses to not being quite sure of his prose. ⁓ Read also prodigiously learned article by Elena Croce on Gracián.[9] Such learning is more overwhelming than entertaining.

15 JANUARY More of Stefan George–Hofmannsthal correspondence, consisting mainly of shoptalk between writers. Reminds me of my disgust for literary society, occasioned by the fact that when I did frequent it in my early years, I heard from Oscar Wilde and his *Gefährten*, including many of the then most noted English and American, no subject discussed except publishing, royalties, or annoyances and difficulties connected with the trade. ⁓ Hofmannsthal as a youth of nineteen serving in the army; has no time for reading, but feels he is getting culture and compensation from contemplating photos of Boecklin, Stuck, and the English Pre-Raphaelites.

[8] The very next year, in fact, the two poets were to be co-founders of the literary journal *Blätter für die Kunst*. Hugo von Hofmannsthal, the Austrian, remained a romantic symbolist throughout his career and wrote for a wide public in theater and opera. George, on the other hand, developed toward an austerely classical and quasi-religious approach, which never gained him wide popular understanding. Their letters were published as *Briefwechsel zwischen George und Hofmannsthal (1891–1906)* (Berlin, 1938).

[9] This article by the daughter of the noted philosopher Benedetto Croce appeared in the September–October, 1941, issue of *Civiltà Moderna*, Florence. Baltasar Gracián y Morales (1601–58), a Spanish philosopher, was expelled from the Jesuit order and confined to a monastery as a result of his *El Criticón*, which has been called "the Spanish *Pilgrim's Progress*."

16 JANUARY Finished Shirer's *Berlin Diary*. Painfully calls up events from day to day which made me so unhappy when they occurred. S. belongs to a new category, the correspondent of the highly influential American daily. Half-Bohemian, shrewd, an intelligent observer, but shallow and easily overflowing with the feelings and judgments of the group-spirit of his own set. He has acquired extraordinary authority, and can afford to treat governments *de puissance à puissance*. Such is the value even the most despotic of regimes put on public opinion. I recall Duranty saying when I questioned his being allowed into Italy that they would not dare refuse a *New York Times* man.

17 JANUARY Finished Hofmannsthal and Stefan George correspondence. Apart from trade matters as to printers and publishers, there are few letters of a personal nature. These betray that G. wanted to absorb H. within himself, and that H. fought hard to avoid his (S. G.'s) parlor. And G.'s task was too precious and exerting, while H. had a hanker for immediate results in a world less awesomely select than G.'s. ～ Began Alain-Fournier's *Le Grand Meaulnes* on insistence of Luigi Franchetti. Cannot yet say how it will please me.[1]

18 JANUARY Pirenne about South Italy's republics and regions. Early history of Venice, succinct and brief, but most satisfactory interpretation. What a contrast to German or German-minded Italian writers, and Italians *are* German-minded. By the way, I have looked over the list of Reclam publications and discovered that Heine and all other Jewish authors have been omitted—all except Spinoza.

[1] Alain-Fournier was the pseudonym of the French symbolist poet Henri Fournier. *Le Grand Meaulnes* (Lausanne, 1913) was his only completed novel.

Presumably, like Shakespeare and Rembrandt, he has been assimilated and Aryanized. Or is it that the learning of the eliminators did not go far enough to tell them that Spinoza was a Jew?

19 JANUARY Finished Ruskin's letters to Norton. Glad to get better acquainted with Ruskin, whom I read little as a youth and not at all since. Struck by his continuous effort to dig into his conscience to discover what he really means and what he should think. Vehement and passionate but not obstinate for long. Tormented by the woes of the world, he was one of the first to trace them to the industrial system. Sees everywhere destruction of ancient beauty in artifacts and even in the sublimity of Mont Blanc. Dares to say what he thinks, even to the extent of harping on his horror of everything American.

20 JANUARY Finished Alain-Fournier's *Le Grand Meaulnes*, first published in 1913. Fascinatingly airy, yet poignant, tragic but tender. Reminds me of *Wuthering Heights*, of Novalis, of Claude Silve's *Jardin vers l'Est*, of Gide's *Faux-Monnayeurs* all in one, and at the same time of Watteau. So unlikely and yet so real—in the realm of ideated reality, I mean. Igor Markewitch tells me about a remarkable correspondence of the author's. He was killed in the First World War, belonged to circle of Péguy, Rivière, etc., etc.[2]

[2] Markewitch, a composer and conductor—Russian-born (1912) and now living in Switzerland—was a wartime guest of the Berensons, occupying what B. B. called a *"villino"* ("little palace") on the grounds of I Tatti. The correspondence he described was a voluminous and vivid one, begun in 1905, with Fournier's *lycée* classmate and future brother-in-law, Jacques Rivière (1886–1925). Rivière was editor of *La Nouvelle Revue Française*. Charles Péguy edited (1900–14) another influential French literary review, *Les Cahiers de la Quinzaine,* and was a poet and essayist of importance.

21 JANUARY To my amazement I came across the following line, the penultimate one in Maximian's first elegy: *"Dura satis miseris memoratio bonorum."* Of this Dante's *"Nessun maggior dolore"* is a transcription.[3] ⁓ Began Bury's *Greek Historians.*[4] Read Bury always with real delight as his mind works like my own. ⁓ Began also the Nazi Koran, *Mein Kampf,* for Hitler, besides much else in common with Mohammed, has given his adherents *a book.*[5]

22 JANUARY Of late *Atlantic Monthly* reached me seldom. Recently a friend in Rome sent me some back numbers containing articles by [A. J.] Nock and by [James] Marshall on anti-Semitism. First sees perils of it in America and then decides that Jews, being Orientals, are unassimilable. Marshall has an easy time contrasting this, but meets the serious question with rhetoric about democracy, and how it would fail if anti-Semitism prevailed, with the implication that it won't prevail. Unhappily, this is by no means certain. ⁓ Charles Morgan, the "exquisite" novelist, in defense of French culture.[6] Excellent on culture, but he

[3] The *Elegiae* of Maximianus Etruscus, a sixth-century (A.D.) Etruscan orator, appear in Volume 7 of *Poetae Latini Minores* (8 vols., Paris, 1824–26). The full lines in Dante's *Inferno* (V, 121–23) are: *"Nessun maggior dolore / Che ricordarsi del tempo felice / Nella miseria. . . ."*

[4] John Bagnell Bury (1861–1927): *The Ancient Greek Historians* (London, 1909). An Irish historian and philologist, Bury was one of the leading modern authorities on the late Roman and Byzantine empires. He taught first at the University of Dublin and then, for twenty-five years, at Cambridge.

[5] Adolf Hitler's *Mein Kampf* was written during his 1924 imprisonment with Rudolph Hess following the Munich "beer-hall putsch."

[6] Among the prize-winning novels of Charles Morgan (1894–    ), long-time drama critic of the *Times* of London, is *The Fountain* (1932).

seems to have no great acquaintance with French fanaticism of the political and religious kind.

23 JANUARY Finished Tarlé's *Napoléon*. The most readable and brilliant story of Napoleon's life that I have read as a grown-up. The Soviet error comes out in his constant reproach that Napoleon would not sacrifice the bourgeois for the proletarian—and by "proletarian" he clearly means the day laborer, not the peasant or artisan. He recognizes that the peasants, except in the Vendée, were favorable to Napoleon, as were the upper- and lower-middle classes, i.e., the great majority of the French people. But "people" to Tarlé means the proletariat, and the others —the majority—can become people only when reduced to being proletarians.

24 JANUARY In bed with a cold, the first serious one in eighteen months. Nicky finished reading aloud Pirenne's luminous and well-articulated account of what happened to the Western world between the sixth and ninth centuries. Delighted with his debunking of the culture and even the civilization of the Carolingians. Always felt it was a flash in the pan and their art a good-little-boy who died at the age of ten. ∽ By myself many pages of Hitler. If the premise is granted that nothing counts except the German people, its welfare, its grandeur, its splendor, and that he is the realization of the perfect German, then what he has to say follows logically and incontrovertibly. He is then the born ruler of the one and only people that counts.

25 JANUARY In bed. Eugene O'Neill's *Strange Interlude* in one sitting. Liked it much more than his *Mourning Becomes Electra*. Technically interesting in giving the thoughts that dash and flutter through the head as well as

the spoken utterances.[7] Characters well developed, never make curious lapses. The heroine a complex and careful and not oversubtle study of a full-blooded female: amorous, masterful, possessive, yet muddle-minded enough to chase after the Blue Bird—happiness as an independent state beyond the satisfaction offered by the exercise of functions. Exhaustion alone brings her peace.

26 JANUARY Nicky read aloud Orlando's book, printed in America, on Roman Question.[8] Abstract part very talmudistic, but accounts of Orlando's personal relation with Vatican significant and human. ⁓ By myself Stephen Crane's *Maggie*—fairly accurate picture of Irish slums in New York, done with economy, precision, and no little art in representation.[9] ⁓ Also more Herodotus, with increasing admiration of his way of presenting history as a field where character and chance play such a great part. Never fails to tell the appropriate and illuminating story. ⁓ More Hitler; am fed up with his accounts of politics in Vienna.

[7] *Strange Interlude* won the Pulitzer Prize in 1928. The nine-act drama reintroduced asides in its exposition of the psychological conflicts and entanglements of its chief characters. The trilogy *Mourning Becomes Electra* was produced three years later; it adapted to nineteenth-century New England the themes of classical Greek drama.

[8] Vittorio Emanuele Orlando (1860–1952): *Rome versus Rome: A Chapter of My War Memoirs* (New York, 1937). The notable jurist had held a number of Cabinet posts and served as Premier (1917–19). An anti-Fascist, he returned to his professorship at the University of Rome in 1945. In B.B.'s memoirs for 1941–44 (*Rumour and Reflection*, 1952), Orlando and members of his family are discussed, and B.B. acknowledges their friendship and help during his period of hiding from the Fascist gangs.

[9] *Maggie: A Girl of the Streets* (1893), regarded as the first American naturalistic novel, was reprinted (with the short stories to which B.B. refers in the Diary entries for the next few days) in *Twenty Stories* (New York, 1940).

27 JANUARY Still in bed. Nicky began to read aloud Voigt's *Wiederbelebung des klassischen Altertums.*[1] I read it almost fifty years ago and remembered it well; recalled it with such pleasure that I promised myself to reread it. Glad to be doing so at last, and turns out to be far beyond what I thought of it when I was less than a third of my present age. ∽ Happy accident brought me Nolhac's beautifully printed Harvard lectures on Petrarch, based on Voigt, very readable.[2] ∽ Stephen Crane's "Experiment in Misery," wonderful portrait of a jolly, shamefree old bum. ∽ More Herodotus, a fine repartee of Andrianus to Themistocles.

28 JANUARY More Herodotus. More Hitler. More stories by Stephen Crane. ∽ A volume of essays, entitled *Arti Figurative,* by Croce.[3] I am constantly surprised by any resemblances in detail and particularly in attitude toward art history, and the more exasperated by something dogmatic, arrogant, supercilious in his tone, as of a pope who alone possessed infallibility, while all the rest of us were contumacious heretics. ∽ Hitler is a Merlin imprisoned in his system as that wizard was by Vivien.

29 JANUARY Nolhac on Petrarch as bibliophile, and more Voigt, to whom Nolhac owes everything except the

[1] Berlin, 1859, 1893. Georg Voigt (1827–91) was the German historian whose brilliant interpretation of the revival of humanism inspired later studies in that field.
[2] Voigt's influence marked the scholarly researches of Pierre de Nolhac (1859–1936), librarian at the Bibliothèque Nationale in Paris, author of *Petrarch and the Ancient World* (1888; Boston, 1907).
[3] Benedetto Croce (1866–1952): *La Critica e la Storia delle Arti Figurative: Questioni di Metodo* (Bari, 1934). Written at various times over the preceding decade, these essays are a small part of Croce's body of work on aesthetics, one of the philosopher-critic's several areas of intense interest.

16

results of further research. ⌒ More Hitler, interesting when writing on interesting affairs, and even intelligent. All he says about colonies surprisingly true. Does he ever ask himself what would happen when Germany made its rule universal and left no chink for outbreaks of wars? What would then become of a humanity which, in his belief, can be kept decent by war alone? ⌒ Began Croce's *Estetica*, which produces to start with a pleasanter impression than his later abstract writings.[4]

30 JANUARY Hitler more realistic than any writer on politics yet encountered—realistic in the sense of knowing how to appeal and to whom to appeal if you want to attain and keep power. ⌒ Gabriele Pepe on early medieval Italy,[5] rather indulgent to clergy, almost delusive about Gregory the Great, full of bitter contempt for the nobility and loathing of the Teutonic invader. ⌒ In Herodotus, all that leads up to Plataea, as detailed and alive as if happening today. How Greek the admiration of the beauty of Masistes.

31 JANUARY Bury's chapter on Herodotus in his *Greek Historians*, nothing like so delightful and sympathetic as [T. R.] Glover's, but as everything else Bury wrote, worth following. Discover, among additions at end of the volume, that he was preparing a book on Catherine II, to me a most unexpected phase of his activity. ⌒ Herodotus' account of Plataea, actual battle in which Mardonius is

[4] Croce's philosophy of art, like his views on a number of other subjects, underwent considerable development and change over his long writing career. Thus, the edition of *Estetica* that B. B. was reading at this time (Bari, 1934) reflects the Croce opinions as set down between 1909 and 1934. Later in this Diary, B. B. comments also on subsequent editions.
[5] *Il Medio evo Barbarico d'Italia* (Torino, 1941, 1945). Pepe (born in 1899) is professor of medieval and modern history at Bari University.

killed, rather scamped, leaves one hungry. ⁓ Stephen Crane's "Open Boat" gives one something of the cosmic feeling about the ocean which seems peculiarly Anglo-Saxon. Conrad, although born a Pole, took it up. Its climax is Melville's *Moby Dick*.

```
┌─────────────────────────────┐
│  ┌───────────────────────┐  │
│  │                       │  │
│  │    February 1942      │  │
│  │  ───────────────────  │  │
│  │  S  M  T  W  T  F  S  │  │
│  │  1  2  3  4  5  6  7  │  │
│  │  8  9  10 11 12 13 14 │  │
│  │  15 16 17 18 19 20 21 │  │
│  │  22 23 24 25 26 27 28 │  │
│  │                       │  │
│  └───────────────────────┘  │
└─────────────────────────────┘
```

1 FEBRUARY Finished Bruno Barilli's *Il Sole in Trappola*,[6] bearing note of a journey to the Cape [of Good Hope] and back through Rhodesia, Somaliland, etc. Singularly free from nationalistic humbug, fresh and amusing. ~ Finished also Stephen Crane's "The Monster," finer even than Ibsen's *Enemy of the People*, because here the people do their best to ruin a man who, out of loyalty and humanity, refuses to discard a person whom they cannot abide in their midst—well written as well as thought out.

2 FEBRUARY Returned to Churchill's *Marlborough*, interrupted owing to Mary's inability to read aloud. It is the most expensive book in history. Winston should not have

---

[6] *Il Sole in Trappola: Diario del Periplo dell'Africa (1931)* (Florence, 1941). Barilli (1880–1952) was an Italian music critic and traveler.

had the leisure to write it, but should have been in office,[7] in which case England would have been so well armed that Germany would not have dared to disobey her, or having done so, would soon have had to yield. As it is, England is spending billions, where tens of millions, or a few hundred millions, would have sufficed. But Anglo-Saxons are not military minded, and will not believe in war until it is upon them.

3 FEBRUARY Mary read aloud a couple of short stories by Mary Webb, prolix and not conceived as short stories—merely episodes she could not use for her novels.[8] ～ Nicky aloud out of Voigt, the chapter on Boccaccio, and began the one on Coluccio Salutati, both brilliantly and zestfully told. Strange that such a book on such a subject has not attracted an English translator. I tried hard enough in earlier years, but no Anglo-American publisher would take it. ～ Have finished Herodotus and begun Arrian.[9] Fear it will seem dull and flat after Herodotus. Looked through several book catalogues, an occupation which rests and amuses me.

4 FEBRUARY Continued Churchill's *Marlborough*. It is always the Lord hardening Pharaoh's heart. This time it is James II, his coming to the throne and his headlong follies, egged on by his confessors and toadies. ～ Read story of a

[7] Sir Winston's biography was written during the first years of his decade of absence from the Cabinet (1929–39).

[8] Her native Shropshire was the background for all five novels of Mary Webb (1881–1927). Her best-known work, *Precious Bane*, won the Femina-Vie Heureuse prize for 1924–5.

[9] Arrian (*c.* 90–180 A.D.) was a Greek historian, philosopher, and general (under the Roman Emperor Hadrian). His *Indica* is the account of the voyage of Nearchus, one of Alexander the Great's generals; his *Anabasis of Alexander*, modeled on Xenophon, is our prime source of information on the Macedonian conqueror.

military complexion by Stephen Crane,[1] charged with the sense of irony in things, *ironica rerum*, and a curious traditional feeling about time and space that haunted American literature all through the nineteenth century. ⁓ Read a chapter of Collingwood's *Life of Ruskin*.[2] Surely Ruskin deserved and should have a more distanced and intelligent biographer.

5 FEBRUARY Commenced Plato, beginning with the *Euthyphro*, and observed to my delight that I could read him much easier than I feared.[3] Can enjoy the irony, the delicate wit, the Jane-Austen-like evenness of the style. ⁓ Mary aloud more of *Marlborough* and how the Lord went on hardening Pharaoh-James II's heart. ⁓ More of Crane, stories in which he tries desperately to write and succeeds, but with occasional misvaluing of words. Pity of pities he died so young! He might have lived to serve as a dike against the avalanche of pseudo realism.

6 FEBRUARY Finished *Euthyphro*. How playful, at times almost arch! How civilized a state of society where such writing was possible. ⁓ More of *Marlborough* and the headlong obstinacy of the Stuart Pharaoh! Curious that violence should have such adherents. I dare say because it seems to succeed so well, and yet few are the cases where it has

[1] As a result of the popularity of his *Red Badge of Courage* (1895), Crane became a war correspondent and had opportunity to see at first hand both the Greco-Turkish conflict of 1896–97 and the Spanish-American War of 1898. His observations are reflected in several of his short stories, as well as in *War Is Kind* (1899), in which he experimented with epigrammatic free verse.

[2] William G. Collingwood (1854–1932): *Life and Works of Ruskin* (2 vols., London, 1893).

[3] *Euthyphro* and the other Platonic writings discussed by B. B. in later Diary entries were read in the eleven-volume Loeb Classical Library edition of Plato's *Complete Works*, which has both Greek text and English translation.

won through in the long run. Perhaps the best case is the history of the Jesuits, always favoring political violence, and yet being today almost as dominant as ever.

7 FEBRUARY Read Thomas Wolfe's *A Portrait of Bascome Hawke,* which reminded me of Melville, of [Ernest] Hello, and of [D. H.] Lawrence. Wonderful pages about Boston and Faneuil Hall Market in the spring, as a youth felt it.[4] Recalled me much that I felt when I used to accompany Mrs. Brooks Adams to market there. At end of story a dreary yet touching and tender picture of old age. All through a cosmic sense of time and tide that haunts American minds. Yet the best in the story has really but a tangential relation to it, and that is the weakness in it and in much American literature of today.

8 FEBRUARY Began Plato's *Apology.* Socrates' plea that he has to meet two kinds of accusers—those present, easy to confront, and those [whose bias is] due to slander or malicious gossip breathed in when youths or even children —applies overwhelmingly to a person like myself and sounds ever-contemporary. So does his saying that the man in the street knows almost more about the artist than the artist himself does. ⁓ Finished "theoretical" part of Croce's *Estetica,* seldom disagreeing in concrete instances, but unable to understand his general theory or, rather, sheer axiom.

9 FEBRUARY After Herodotus, wanting to get a comprehensive idea of Persia as known to the ancients, I turned to Eduard Meyer and began to read the third chapter

---

[4] The Boston setting in Wolfe's short novel is based on his experience of that city while studying for his M.A. degree at Harvard (1922).

of his fourth volume.[5] I find him always more satisfactory than anybody else on any historical subject. ∽ More of Plato's *Apology.* How contemporary, how eternal in a sense his Socrates is, more likely to survive than the Jesus of the Synoptic Gospels—so enigmatic, so pietistic, so ultra-human. ∽ Voigt's account of San Ciriaco of Ancona, about whom I discovered a good deal myself pioneering among Italian fifteenth- and sixteenth-century pictures all over the world.

10 FEBRUARY Went on with *Mein Kampf.* All he says about propaganda profoundly true, but he does not realize that it has been deliberately practiced for many ages by Holy Church. The kind of propaganda the Germans had during the last war may have been ineffective at home, as he complains, but it was most successful abroad, as I can witness. ∽ Finished Stephen Crane's short stories. Having almost Dante's or Tolstoi's gift of making one see the people and scenes he describes. His stories about small boys convey their psychology to sheer perfection—their pretenses, their make-believes, etc.

11 FEBRUARY Finished *Apology* and began *Crito,* and for the first time in all but sixty years returned to the Psalms in Hebrew. To my surprise and delight I could read quite easily. I do not flatter myself that this means very much, for one does know the Psalms nearly by heart in Eng-

[5] B. B. read Meyer's *Geschichte des Altertums* in the four-volume Stuttgart edition of 1939. The work was begun by Meyer in 1884 and had gone through several revisions before his death in 1930; it was a book the great German historian had never been able to finish: each new development in archeology or anthropology or comparative philology provided him with material for fresh changes. His emphasis on primary sources and on the interdependence of all civilizations carried forward the traditions of Ranke and of Barthold Niebuhr.

lish and in Latin. So it is easy to follow the Hebrew. ⏤ Read *Asiatica*, a monthly Italian review of Asiatic affairs in imitation of the American *Asia*—only the Italian affair is official and sheer propaganda. Last number foresaw simultaneous fall of both Singapore and Gibraltar, with the consequent and irremediable ruin of the British Empire.

12 FEBRUARY Finished a book by Elio Vittorini giving account of his return to his native village in Sicily and to his mother, very repetitive, although not exactly *à la* Gertrude Stein, and pathetic but in a rough, almost brutal way.[6] ⏤ More Plato, more Hitler, more of G. Pepe's history of early medieval Italy. Hitler's account of German revolution in November, 1918, almost touching, but scarcely historical. What a belief that the great masses are pails into which you can pour any kind of slop that you want to go to their heads, and make them act like your golems!

13 FEBRUARY Marlborough's troubled years under William and Mary's displeasure. Winston makes a good defense. ⏤ Hitler begins to be aware that he is at once a seer and a statesman—the rarest, as he says, and the most dynamic of all associations in one and the same person. ⏤ Croce's account in his *Estetica* of Vico,[7] who certainly was a full precursor of serious thinking on the subject, but far beyond Croce's own. ⏤ Nearly finished Pepe's laborious

[6] *Conversazione in Sicilia* (1941) appeared in America under the title *In Sicily*, with an introduction by Ernest Hemingway. Vittorini (1909–    ) has exercised an important influence in Italy for some years as an editor and also as a translator of contemporary American works.

[7] Giovanni Battista (Giambattista) Vico (1668–1744) was an Italian philosopher, whose *New Science* applied a theory of cyclical development not only to the study of history but also to that of aesthetics and law. Long ignored, his thought has had a profound influence on modern historians and literary figures. The effect has been especially great in Italy through Croce's works.

but invaluable book on the barbarian occupation of Italy from the end of the sixth century to Charlemagne.

14 FEBRUARY Hitler, when he first wrote *Mein Kampf*, deplores the idea of turning Germany into a great factory and of proletarianizing her people! ⁓ Plato's *Phaedo* begins charmingly, of course, but with arguments to my sense somewhat farfetched. ⁓ More of Marlborough. Winston's able defense against charges of disloyalty and double-dealing. Calumny is certainly in great form, and I fear it can be said *"Magna est calumnia et prevalebit."* That certainly is the case with whomever the Church in the earlier Middle Ages has calumniated!

15 FEBRUARY Socrates is reported as having said [8] that real philosophers study nothing at all but dying and being dead; that they find no pleasure in eating, drinking, and love-making; that they despise the care of the body, fine clothes and shoes, and personal adornment; and that they think of nothing but the soul. In all this and in his longing to get away from the body to give the soul a chance by itself, Socrates was preparing the way for asceticism and for monastic as well as Puritan Christianity. ⁓ Hitler rages against a free press and insists that it is the state that must control it as it controls education of the young, the press continuing their education as governess. He does not realize that the suppression of organs of publicity has been tried often enough!

16 FEBRUARY The argument for pre-existence of the soul and its continuance after the death of the body (*Phaedo*) is eventually based on the naïve idea of reminiscence, for otherwise how could we recognize anything as

[8] In Plato's *Phaedo* (64, 65).

25

being what it is. I am curious to see whether Plato ever develops the question of resemblance, and how we know that one thing is identical with another.

17 FEBRUARY Winston's defense of Marlborough and others of the day against double-dealing in keeping up relations with James II proves how mighty is calumny, and how likely to win through unless and until it encounters some David to bring it to nought. These calumnies have lasted till Winston unravels and blows them away one by one. Strange that no one previously took the trouble. But it is human to accept adverse gossip uncritically. Indeed calumny is based on that fact. ∼ Read about Socrates in Joel's *"Vorsokratiker,"* [9] wordy but interesting.

18 FEBRUARY Hitler deplores the proletarization of cities that hitherto had been cultural centers. I wholeheartedly agree with his regretting populations being attached to their towns as peasants to their glebe, and not as in Rome of today—and, indeed, all past days. ∼ Found in *Phaedo* parallels to the doctrine of karma, as well as speculative talk I used to hear as a youth about the earth-haunted soul being loath to tear itself from this world, and continuing to haunt it as a ghost.

19 FEBRUARY Finished first volume of Churchill's *Marlborough*, with account of King's death. Now the fun begins, I suppose. ∼ More of *Phaedo*. How touching and human when Socrates stops talking and a silence falls upon all. Then Phaedo tells how Socrates used to love to stroke his hair. ∼ Voigt on humanism in Siena, where it had little

[9] In *Geschichte der antiken Philosophie*, Vol. I (Tubingen, 1921). Karl Joel (1864-1920) was professor of classical philosophy at Basel University.

chance because of the turbulence of the political situation, and of Venice, where all were occupied in serving the state to the extent of having no leisure for the free exercise of the mind. ⁓ More Hitler, now beginning his theories of race.

20 FEBRUARY In *Mein Kampf*, terrible effect of an idea like Gobineau's narrowed down in Wagner and Chamberlain, and canalized into the most fanatical Jew-baiting the world has ever known.[1] ⁓ In *Phaedo*, such convincing presence of Socrates, the way he stops talking to brood and meditate. The argument for immortality, although specious, so beautifully conducted. ⁓ Finished Joel's account of Socrates in his *"Vorsokratiker."* If only Joel could say clearly what he had to say, without pathos and ejaculations.

21 FEBRUARY Reading Hitler, I am more and more puzzled if indeed *Mein Kampf* is his unassisted personal experience. But for Judaeophobia, which is at the bottom of his race-madness, he has deeper and clearer things to say about politics, whether social or international, than most writers, than most German writers certainly. He dares, he a German, to go so far as to say that the state is not an ultimate, although it should serve the *race*, but still it is a tremendous proof of independence of thought on the part of any German who is not a declared anarchist.

22 FEBRUARY Several chapters of Collingwood's *Ruskin.* Tame and unevocative, a mere lifeless chronicle. He

[1] Joseph Arthur, comte de Gobineau (1816–82), who wrote on "the inequality of human races" in 1853, was a principal early exponent of "Nordic supremacy." Houston Stewart Chamberlain (1855–1927), the son of a British admiral, settled in Germany and married the daughter of Richard Wagner. Wagner, of course, was preoccupied throughout his life with the themes of German mythology and with the dedication to extreme nationalism. His son-in-law's principal work, *Foundations of the Nineteenth Century* (1899), was a major document of Teutonic glorification.

avoids to the utmost Ruskin's marriage and annulment. How incomparably more one gets out of Ruskin's letters to Norton, where the character, the passion, the earnestness, the sincerity of the man shines out so clearly. ∼ Looked at various art books for their illustrations: one on Johann Liss,[2] one on the St. George Church at Cologne,[3] another on the Pigorini seals and on engraved stones and bronzes.[4]

23 FEBRUARY Finished the *Phaedo*. Disappointed by its arguments and by the vision of the other world, but simply captivated by the atmosphere and the incomparable description of the last moments of Socrates. ∼ More Hitler with admiration and despair. ∼ Croce's second version of his *Estetica*,[5] very superior to first, but still! What if art is intuition, and all language poetry? "Where everyone is somebody, then no one's anybody." What profits it if Croce is right!

24 FEBRUARY Began the *Phaedrus*. How idyllic, but with no touch of the *faux bon*, not even as little as in Theocritus, in the description of the out-of-doors and personages. Pity the novel was not invented. What a novelist Plato would have made! ∼ *Mein Kampf*—almost everything about international relations would be admirable but for his Marxian attitude toward international finance and its

[2] R. Oldenburg: *Jan Lys* (Rome, 1921). Lys (also referred to as Liss, Lis, or Van der Lys) was a German painter. He was born about 1570 and died in 1629. Influenced by Caravaggio, he was active in Rome and Venice.

[3] W. Schorn and A. Verbeek: *Die St. Georgs-Kirche in Koln* (Berlin, 1940).

[4] Francesco Ficoroni: *Gemmae Antiquae Litterae aliasque Rariares Accerunt Vetera Monumenta* (Rome, 1798). Ficoroni (1664-1747) was a collector and student of classical art.

[5] Bari, 1940.

identification with Jewry, which he assumes as an indisputable fact. Japan alone is invulnerable to attack of Jewry!

25 FEBRUARY Looked through a new book on Baldung's drawings.[6] They give him away as a clever imitator of Dürer as a draftsman, but never once attaining the movement of his line. ~ Getting toward end of *Mein Kampf*, and Hitler's foreign policy as he then conceived it. How often I have deplored that there were not enough Greeks in antiquity to Hellenize Italy at least, and likewise that there were not enough Germans to Germanize the territories of the Vistula and farther east and south. Hitler's dream is to do it now!

26 FEBRUARY Finished Collingwood's *Ruskin*, a dull, lifeless book giving no portrait of the man, no touch of life, only facts (not all), events, testimonies, etc. Nothing like the impression one gets from Ruskin's letters to Norton, where is revealed a disintegrated soul in a torment of doubt, and a passion for sincerity. Pity such a quasi-Dostoevskian Englishman has not yet found his biographer.

27 FEBRUARY Finished *Mein Kampf*, as interesting a political work as I have ever read, and from the usual Continental nationalistic point of view, more genuine, more perspicacious, clearer and deeper. All brought to nought by the conviction that the supreme enemy is the Jew. That is bound to bring him low, not because he is so madly prejudiced, but because he is fighting windmills, while the real

[6] Carl Koch: *Hans Baldung Grien* (Berlin, 1941). Baldung (*c.* 1480–1545) painted religious and mythological subjects and some portraits, as well as producing woodcuts and designs for stained glass. He was court painter to the Bishop of Strasbourg. "Grien" or "Grün" is sometimes added to his name because of his predilection for the color green in his paintings.

enemy is busy attacking him. If the Jew is as omnipotent as Hitler sees him, then, being the *"Real-Politiker"* that he is, he should come to terms with him, seeing that he cannot erase him, except temporarily in Germany and in the countries he is momentarily occupying.

28  FEBRUARY  Began Robert d'Harcourt's *La Jeunesse de Schiller*. What a relief to read a Frenchman on any literary or artistic subject, after reading, as is my lot, so much German or even Italian! Interesting portrait of Karl-Eugen, the ruler of Württemberg, and how absolutely submissive, voluptuously so, to his will [his subjects were].[7] Is it to be wondered that Germans delight in submission, when they have practiced it from eternity with no interruption? For their efforts at liberation have not been from submissiveness as a principle, but only from submissiveness to hereditary rulers. ∼ Got to Nicholas V in Voigt. Reading him again after so long I rejoice to discover how much of Voigt I remember, and even more, how much of him remains in me behind memory, forming a humus, as it were, out of which has grown so much that I have felt and said about the Renaissance. I often am tempted to believe that what really fecundates one is not what one actually remembers but what one can no longer recall, just because it has become part and parcel of ourselves. ∼ Aristides speaks in the Platonian *Theages*, 130 D-E: "I will tell you Socrates what is incredible. . . . For I never learnt anything from you, as you

---

[7] Robert d'Harcourt (1881–    ): *La Jeunesse de Schiller* (Paris, 1928). Friedrich Schiller had his own personal experience of the Duke of Württemberg's tyranny: son of an army surgeon, he was forced to attend the Duke's military school, and after he had studied medicine at Stuttgart, became an army doctor at Karl-Eugen's insistence. His first play, *Die Raüber*, was performed when the young doctor was only twenty-three; a drama of protest against society's injustice, it led to his fleeing from Stuttgart and his monarch's anger.

know yourself; but I made progress, whenever I was with you, if I was merely in the same house, without being in the same room, but more progress, when I was in the same room. And it seemed to be much more when I was in the same room and looked at you as you were speaking, than when I turned my eyes elsewhere: but my progress was far the greatest and much marked whenever I sat beside you and held and touched you." When Ben Nicholson went away, he wrote that although he had almost never heard me speak of art, he had, during the months he had passed with us, learned more about it than he had ever acquired elsewhere.[8]

[8] Nicholson (1894–    ), a British painter, is represented in the Tate Gallery, New York's Museum of Modern Art, and other leading museums. He has written monographs and edited an art magazine.

# March 1942

| S | M | T | W | T | F | S |
|---|---|---|---|---|---|---|
| 1 | 2 | 3 | 4 | 5 | 6 | 7 |
| 8 | 9 | 10 | 11 | 12 | 13 | 14 |
| 15 | 16 | 17 | 18 | 19 | 20 | 21 |
| 22/29 | 23/30 | 24/31 | 25 | 26 | 27 | 28 |

1 MARCH The years preceding Blenheim, and how Marlborough's patience was tried, at home by the "little-Englander" navalists and appeasers, and abroad by the Dutch flatly refusing to risk battle. Reading all this makes me appreciate how carefully I obeyed my instinct to have nothing to do where I would depend on convincing and persuading others. I could not have stood it, for which reason there is nothing I admire so much in Marlborough as his patience with all and sundry.

2 MARCH Robert d'Harcourt's *La Jeunesse de Schiller* teaches me a great deal I did not know. In fact, I took no interest in that writer from my boyhood till last spring. I discover now that physically and intellectually he was singularly like Shelley. He was far more eloquent, but for that very reason never reaches the heights occasionally reached by the English aristocrat. Would the latter have

survived to be known if submitted to as dreadful difficulties? [9]

3 MARCH When I have for many years been encountering references to a person, plan, idea, or theme of any sort, but out of inertia or better reasons could not or did not hasten to read up on it, gathering curiosity at last overflows, and I then enjoy a comprehensive book on the subject as I am now enjoying D'Harcourt's *Schiller*, enjoying it perhaps out of proportion to its intrinsic merits, just because it satisfies my hunger.

4 MARCH Finished D'Harcourt's *Schiller*. There is likeness not only in physique and habits between Schiller and Shelley (excepting snuff) but also in outlook and thought. D'Harcourt says he leaves Schiller where he ceases to be the poet and turns more and more to history and philosophy. Stefan George says the exact opposite—namely that it is a mistake to take Schiller for a poet, and that his real greatness was as aesthetician and thinker on art!

5 MARCH Ricarda Huch on German romantics.[1] Although I am now reading it in French, and although she is one of the best of German writers, one feels after reading D'Harcourt's *Schiller* as if plunged into a grittier, cloudier,

[9] Schiller's life was indeed a difficult one. After fleeing from Stuttgart, he completed two tragic dramas; he settled briefly in Mannheim, but was soon in financial difficulty, and went on, in rapid succession, to Leipzig and Dresden, writing all the while. He spent four years as a professor of history at Jena, until illness forced his retirement. In the remaining years (he died in 1805 at forty-six), he wrote his greatest dramas and established his reputation as one of the founders of modern German literature.

[1] *Les Romantiques Allemands* (Paris, 1933) was translated from *Die Blütezeit der Romantik* (1899). Ricarda Huch (1864–1947) wrote literary studies in addition to her own works in fiction.

more confusing atmosphere. She refers to much she leaves unexplained, she syncopates, she makes sudden springs— and yet she is so moderate and so classical compared to most writers of her race who treat nowadays of any question of literature, art, and even history.

6 MARCH In Winston's *Marlborough*, the days preceding Blenheim. What Marlborough did was exactly of the same nature as what the Germans have done recently in the Low Countries and France, namely to attack in an utterly unexpected way, and with an unexpected approach to the problem. Too much made by his historians of *morale* and too little of brains—brains finding new ways and means, new instruments of warfare, or such as the adversary lacks. Every conquest in history can be attributed to the same causes.

7 MARCH Turned the pages of Franz Neubert's *Goethe und sein Kreis*,[2] and was confirmed in my conclusion of long ago that there is no such thing as a real likeness of a person. When we have only one portrait, we naïvely imagine it to be a likeness. The moment we have a number, they resemble each other (as in the case of Goethe), so that we can get no clear idea of what the sitter really looked like. So much is this the case that great rulers have had their portraits stereotyped into a convention, as with Ramses the Great, Augustus, and Napoleon, and even a Napoleon III or Victor Emmanuel—and all the popes, of course.

8 MARCH Ricarda Huch on German romantics. What a lot of adolescents destined never to grow up, not

[2] Neubert (1878–*c*.1927) edited anthologies and dictionaries. His *Goethe und sein Kreis* (Leipzig, 1919) is a collection of 651 illustrations of people and places connected with Goethe and his time.

even in old age, despite appearance. That, of course, is their charm and the thrill they give us, and the inspiration they still can be when we abandon our minds to them. As a coterie, the world has never seen anything quite so keen and so creative since antiquity. Amazing what we still owe them. Only the machine-romanticism of today may, if it succeeds, cast them into oblivion.

9 MARCH Ricarda Huch claims that it was the romantics who enmeshed Leonardo in that haze of mystery and magic which led to Pater's *tirade* about the "Mona Lisa." ³ What a fascinating company it was—the Schlegels, with Caroline, Schelling, Tieck, Novalis; farther off Goethe; closer but colder, Schiller; and the philosophers, Fichte and Hegel.⁴ The world has seldom seen the like, on that height, of that quality, and with as much camaraderie, perhaps never before or since the Athens of Socrates and Plato.

10 MARCH Looked through Jirmounsky's *Portugais Primitifs.*⁵ The illustrations suggest all sorts of problems which the writer does not treat at all. On the other hand, he

³ Walter Pater (1839–94) was the Oxford scholar, essayist, and critic. His enthusiastic pages about "Mona Lisa" appear in his essay on Leonardo da Vinci in *The Renaissance* (London, 1888).
⁴ The members of this "fascinating company" were the leaders in the first German romantic movement. Many of them were close friends through their associations at the University of Jena, with the added ties of family relationships—further complicated by Caroline Böhmer's marriages, first to one of the Schlegels and later to Schelling. Although Rousseau in France is acknowledged to be the father of romanticism, these poets, novelists, and idealistic philosophers—all in revolt against eighteenth-century canons of neoclassicism—represented the first organized manifestation of the movement.
⁵ Myron Malkiel-Jirmounsky (1890–    ): *Problèmes des Primitifs Portugais* (Coimbra, 1941). The author taught art history, first at St. Petersburg and then at the Sorbonne; since 1941, he has lectured at the National Museum, Lisbon.

35

makes elaborate diagrams of diagonals he descries in the pictures, and speaks a good deal of *"Geistesgeschichte"*; he quotes Plotinus, etc., etc. ⌒ More of Ricarda Huch on the German romantics, who fascinate me every time I can afford the leisure to abandon my mind to them. ⌒ More too of Winston's *Marlborough* and the difficulties with the caution, the jealousy, and the stupidity of his allies.

I I  MARCH  Finished Ricarda Huch's *Romantiques*. She insists on the impression A. W. Schlegel made as an elegant, brilliant, rather dandiacal and irresistible *charmeur*.[6] She did not know [Mme] de Pange's book on Schlegel and Mme de Staël,[7] where the same personage appears as a heavy, awkward, tactless, pedantic German, something between a figure of fun and one to inspire pity. The difference in appreciation opens up depths of difference between French and German culture at the end of the eighteenth and the beginning of the nineteenth centuries.

I 2  MARCH  Ruskin's *Aratra Pentelici*,[8] full of penetrating glimpses, and of proofs of wide and scholarly reading, but lost in a batter of irrelevancies. Yet how not admire his courage—the way he speaks of a nation ceasing to be

---

[6] August Wilhelm von Schlegel (1767–1845)—poet, translator, critic—edited the literary journal *Athenaeum* with his brother Friedrich and later taught at Bonn. He was married to Caroline Böhmer from 1796 to 1802.

[7] Pauline Laure-Marie (de Broglie), comtesse de Pange (born 1888): *Auguste-Guillaume Schlegel et Madame de Staël* (Paris, 1938). The countess based her book on previously unpublished documents and on the correspondence of her ancestress (whose daughter married one of the distinguished Ducs de Broglie). Mme de Staël (Germaine Necker, baronne de Staël-Holstein; 1766–1817) was the influential Swiss-French woman of letters whose salon was a political and intellectual center.

[8] *Aratra Pentelici* (Orpington, 1879) consists of six Ruskin lectures on sculpture delivered in 1871.

Christian without hurt to itself provided it has character, the way he attacks the worship of Mammon and material civilization in general, and the daring of his prophecies—so overwhelmed, alas, by what is now happening!

13 MARCH Finished Croce's *Nuovi Saggi di Estetica.*[9] Puzzled still why he makes such a fuss about art creation being both spontaneous and mental. Both seem obvious, but so general as to come under the rubric of "where everyone is somebody, then no one's anybody." Nor can I understand his insistence that this statement of his is science and philosophy, and that previous study of the subject has never been. On the other hand, all his utterances both on method and on concrete appreciation meet with "my highest approval."

14 MARCH Difficult to follow Ruskin. One must never forget that sculpture is athletic. But the head counts more than the body. Speaking of Michelangelo and Tintoretto, it is the latter who sees things in the round, whereas the other sees them more as a painter, although he is no master of the craft either on panel or fresco. One thing I do like is his coming out so clearly for oil-painting. As for Michelangelo, Ruskin leaves him no leg to stand on, no more than Leonardo or, for that matter, Raphael!

15 MARCH Started reading Bosanquet's *History of Aesthetic.*[1] Tried to read it when first published in 1892 but it bored me, because it was then so remote from and so irrelevant to my curiosities of that time. Now having read

[9] *Nuovi Saggi di Estetica* (Bari, 1926) is a collection of essays written between 1913 and 1922.
[1] Bernard Bosanquet (1848–1923), English philosopher, represents the idealistic reaction to British empiricism.

37

Croce, I find Bosanquet so fair, frank, and provident in all his definitions and premises that he confers confidence, and his historical allowance always helps him to be fair to the author he is discussing. ∼ Read some of Caroline's letters,[2] and heard Mary read more of *Marlborough*, to the eve of Ramillies.

16 MARCH Ruskin in *Crown of Wild Olive*, admirable on war.[3] What would he have had to say if he were alive now, and war completely militarized! Equally admirable in description of heavy and great industries and their consequences. But a voice crying in the wilderness, not only because there was nobody to bother but also because there was no turning back. Steam was already lord and master, and a relatively limited monarch compared with its successors, all the conquests of electricity and rays.

17 MARCH Began Ruskin's *Lectures on Art*,[4] delighted with all he says on art and religion and his courage in saying it. ∼ Went on with Bosanquet, refreshing in his keeping his narrative clear from arguments in favor of his own private perspective, and reserving criticism till as objective a presentation as possible of the ideas he is writing about. ∼ More of Caroline's letters, continue to be struck by her inner maturity, reminding me of how bemused and unaware of myself I was at the same age.

[2] *Briefe aus der Frühromantik* (2 vols., Leipzig, 1913) includes correspondence from 1778, when Caroline Böhmer, the gifted inspirer of the early German romantic circle, was only fifteen, to her death in 1809. It covers the period of her marriage to August Wilhelm Schlegel, their divorce, and her subsequent marriage to Schelling.
[3] Oxford, 1870. The work was actually completed somewhat earlier, in the year following the end of the American Civil War.
[4] Oxford, 1870.

18 MARCH How little our romantic view of the Italian Renaissance touched the Italian people may be inferred from such a fact as the contrast between the popularity of the humanists and the popularity of their opponents, the Observantists, calling themselves *"Gesuati"* and in many ways precursors of the Jesuits. Probably no house in Siena toward 1450 without a portrait of San Bernardino. Who in Siena and even elsewhere in central Italy did not know all about him and how he looked? How many of those as much as heard of Filelfo, Poggio, Valle, or any of their other humanist contemporaries? What we regard as Renaissance passed entirely over the heads of all but some few thousands of Italians of mid-*quattrocento.*

19 MARCH In the *Deutsche Biographie,* the article on Schelling and his Caroline. The one on Schelling is detailed enough to give one the idea of a genius for skyrocketing ideas which he could not bring down to propositions he could develop. These stimulated others, even his teachers like Fichte and an older fellow student Hegel. Accusing them of plagiarism, he quarreled with both, and ultimately sank into a torpor not unlike that of his English parallel, Coleridge.[5]

[5] Friedrich Wilhelm von Schelling (1775–1854) was one of the founders of the romantic movement in philosophy as a young professor at Jena. The impact of his five-year stay there was influential on all of the members of the "Jena circle." Johann Gottlieb Fichte (1762–1814) left Jena about the same time as Schelling (1803) because of charges of atheism. He went on to establish a career as a philosopher and political liberal in Berlin. Georg Wilhelm Friedrich Hegel (1770–1831) stayed on at Jena for a number of years, before his professorship at Berlin. His philosophy soon developed along utterly different lines from the earlier Schelling influence; indeed, in 1841, the latter was brought to Berlin in an unsuccessful effort to combat the rational dialectical Hegelian trend. Samuel Taylor Coleridge (1772–1834) visited Germany in 1799–1800, and brought back to England a Schiller translation and many of the ideas of the Jena philosophers.

20 MARCH In *Deutsche Biographie*, article on Schleiermacher, whose philological work had a great attraction for me when I was an undergraduate.[6] He seems to have had a dreadful time in Prague, where he, perhaps the greatest Slavist that ever lived, suffered every kind of big and little persecution from the Catholic clergy. ~ More of Caroline's letters, ever more mature in her insight into human nature. ~ Also more Bosanquet, truly meritorious, although too obsequious to William Morris[7] and Pater.

21 MARCH Took up Plato's *Cratylus*. Full of comic and absurd etymologies of the kind that raged till about a century ago. But also half-conscious essays about semantics of a very interesting kind. The miracle is that soon after 400 B.C. there was a community with disinterested mental leisure to ponder over such nonutilitarian matters. Where else were problems discussed so remote from daily needs and from anguish about the future? ~ More Bosanquet, good historical account of late antiquity verging into earliest Middle Ages.

22 MARCH In *Deutsche Biographie*, article on August Wilhelm Schlegel, a gilded mediocrity, but coming in the right time, he served as one of the principal creators of the cultural *Weltanschauung* of the nineteenth century, and indeed of today, to the extent that we still care for literature and art and for thinking about them. He started interest among the northern people in Italian and Spanish literature,

---

[6] Friedrich Daniel Ernst Schleiermacher (1768–1834) was a German Protestant theologian, philologist, and philosopher. Through his friendship with Schelling, Tieck, and Fichte, he was influenced by the romantic movement.

[7] William Morris (1834–96), a contemporary of Walter Pater, was a Pre-Raphaelite medievalist influenced by Ruskin's works; he was an essayist, poet, designer and decorator, and fine printer.

in Indian literature, in philosophy, in analysis of literature of every kind. Yet, in life, there was something heavy and even ridiculous about him, as comes out in Mme de Pange's book about him and Mme de Staël.[8]

23 MARCH "A thing which is different from another does not have to become different from that which is already different, it must have become different from that which is already different, it must have become different from that which has become so, it will have to be different from that which will be so, but from that which is becoming different, it cannot have become, nor can it be going to be, nor can it already be different, it must become different and that is all." The above is not from Gertrude Stein but is taken from among similar passages in the *Parmenides*, which some thinkers rank as Plato's masterpiece. I confess it has made me dizzy to try to follow it, although the Greek lends itself better to such writing than English does.

24 MARCH Finishing Plato's *Cratylus*, it occurred to me that the kind of quibbling that went on there self-consciously dominated and guided much of Indian philosophy (if memory does not betray me, for it is long, long ago since I read any) and even more of Jewish, Moslem, and German mysticism and of so much enmeshing in word entanglements and in phrase nets out of which people lacked the brains to free themselves. What fun though it must have been for the stout Cortes who first explored this seemingly shoreless Pacific of verbiage.

25 MARCH Read into [Plato's] farcical *Hippias Major*, where Socrates mercilessly quizzes a fashionable lecturer. He asks whether he had success in Sparta. Yes, but

[8] See Note 7 for March 11.

41

only in telling them of their genealogies, and the story of their settlements. I am reminded of an acquaintance who wormed his way into exaltedly heraldic British circles by reading up on their family trees and discoursing about them in a flattering way. They were overwhelmed, thinking that if he knew so much about them, how much more he must know about more serious matters, for the British aristocrat of today does not take his origin too seriously.

26 MARCH What dreadful stuff real history presents to view: all the jealousies, envies, spites, vanities, obstinacy, vindictiveness of human nature. This *à propos* of Churchill's life of Marlborough, now concerned with Harley, Mrs. Masham, and the conspiracies to separate him from Anne.[9] The raw material of history has for its principal ingredient human nature. To understand history, one must have that in view, and be aware also that history is not the philosophy of interest, with which it is often confused nowadays.

27 MARCH Nicky read aloud a "Life of Rostoptchine," by a Ségur grandson, who makes him out a willful, but loyal and vital, personality. Tells a good deal about Paul I from Rostoptchine's papers; [1] Paul seems to have

[9] The personal struggles for Queen Anne's influence (and consequent political power) were endless and complex. Sarah Churchill, the general's wife, had been Anne's attendant and close friend for many years. Sarah's cousin, Mrs. Masham, became an attendant later; she gradually supplanted Sarah (now a duchess) in the Queen's favor and, at this period (1708–10), advanced the cause of her kinsman Robert Harley, a Tory leader, in his rivalry with Marlborough.

[1] *Vie du comte Rostoptchine* (Paris, 1871) is the work of Comte A. de Ségur, whose ancestor was one of Napoleon's generals in his Russian invasion. His subject, whose daughter later married into the Ségur family, was Count Feodor Rostoptchine (1763–1824), Governor-General of Moscow in 1812 and leader of its defense—indeed, the man accused of ordering it burned to expel Napoleon.

42

been the legitimate father of Nicholas I. ~ Approaching
with regret the end of Voigt's *Wiederbelebung*, which I
have enjoyed ever so much more this time than on first reading it at least fifty years ago. ~ Disappointed to learn, from
[Wilhelm] Dilthey's article in *Deutsche Biographie* about
Schelling, how theological and nationalistic he was—two
for me *überwundene Standpunkte.*

28 MARCH Reading Goethe's pleasant but rather
pedestrian account of Winckelmann led me to Pater's article
in his *Renaissance.*[2] Writing when Ruskin, William Morris,
and their like were supreme in England, Pater writes about
Winckelmann in a way that for depth, subtlety, and historical perspective surpasses anything done before or since in
any other language. How unconscious I was of the merits of
this essay when I read it as a youth. Happily I understood
and was inspired by his "Epilogue to the Renaissance,"
which became part of my mind.

29 MARCH In "Life of Rostoptchine," the burning
of Moscow. If the French in June, 1940, had let the Germans destroy Paris! The French were too far from nomadic
life, too civilized, for such heroic action. They should then
take thought of all therein implied. ~ Although Bosanquet
restates Kant nontechnically, I get beyond my depth, and
no longer know whether I do or do not understand. Yet I

[2] Goethe's essay was written in 1805 and appears in *Schriften zur
Kunst,* in his complete works. Pater's essay, written in 1873, appears
in *The Renaissance* (London, 1888). Johann Joachim Winckelmann (1717–68) was the German archeologist who greatly inspired the classical revival of the eighteenth and early nineteenth
centuries. He was the first to apply scientific methods to the study
of ancient monuments. Goethe (1749–1832) was interested in
Winckelmann as a result of his own studies of drawing and painting, as well as of his enthusiasm for the classical ideal.

am fascinated, and would like to follow Kant's reasoning. ~ In *Marlborough,* more and more obstinacy and stupidity on part of Anne, domineering querulousness on part of Sarah, timidity on part of the Dutch, and failing hope on part of the Duke himself.

30 MARCH Finished *Hippias Minor,* after reading *Hippias Major.* No possible question but that the latter is a deliberate parody and grotesque caricature of the Sophists, so ironically but never grossly described in *Hippias Minor.* Delighted to discover that Plato anticipated me so long ago in my contention that nobody is so dangerous as the homicidal fool, the honest mischief-maker, the sincere fanatic, the brainless supporter of evil, which he can never recognize for what it is till it has drained him. Give me a self-aware villain every time in preference. With him one can bargain; one can buy him off, make it worth his while to be good by paying him a better reward than his evil course would fetch. With the self-appreciating, good, stupid men there is nothing to be done. As Schiller said, even the gods fight with them in vain. How modern Plato is, not only in his style and procedure but even in the problems discussed! We say "modern," but perhaps neither subject matter nor manner would have existed but for him, and we today still are his close followers. The author of *Hippias Major* has a clever invention, a character whom Socrates makes talk about Hippias in the latter's presence in a way that would be too rude for Socrates himself to do. It is the procedure discovered by Gertrude Stein, but she makes Miss Toklas praise her, Gertrude, for ever and again, and thus avoids the odium of praising herself.[3]

[3] Miss Stein employed this device in her *Autobiography of Alice B. Toklas* (1933), a book of memoirs purporting to be written by her long-time secretary-companion.

44

## April 1942

| S | M | T | W | T | F | S |
|---|---|---|---|---|---|---|
|   |   |   |   | 1 | 2 | 3 | 4 |
| 5 | 6 | 7 | 8 | 9 | 10 | 11 |
| 12 | 13 | 14 | 15 | 16 | 17 | 18 |
| 19/26 | 20/27 | 21/28 | 22/29 | 23/30 | 24 | 25 |

1 APRIL  Finished Ségur's *Rostoptchine*. Something boyish about him to the end, as there must have been about Bismarck too, both loving to show off their brilliancy, and enjoying their own talk. ⁓ Pitiable account of the humanists' world in Voigt—their venality, mendicacy, impudence, quarrelsomeness. As pitiful the result. Their great achievement is buried deep at the foundation of our civilization, and hidden from view, whereas even third-rate artists are known today to an ever larger public of admirers.

2 APRIL  Bosanquet on Schelling, in whom I find anticipation of my way of looking at art; but when he comes down to concrete cases, his admiration is boundless for Guido Reni.[4] ⁓ Read most of a sort of introduction by

[4] Guido Reni (1575–1642) was a rival of Caravaggio. Examples of his work are in the Vatican, the Corsini Gallery in Rome, the Louvre, and a number of Italian churches. In earlier periods, he was often considered one of the Great Masters of all time.

45

Hegel to his aesthetic,[5] as an appendix to Bosanquet. Perhaps the technique of philosophizing requires him to use language and dialectics to say in several thousand words what surely could be said better in as many hundreds. What I can grasp I agree with; at all events, I am driven by curiosity to go on.

3 APRIL Hegel, quoted by Bosanquet, says that architecture has "purified the external world and enclosed it with symmetrical order and affinity to mind." I have felt this ever since I can remember, and more and more consciously. That is why I always loved great terraces, as at Versailles or, better still, at Phaistos [in Crete], introducing an order into the pell-mell of nature, and giving it an ordered base. It is the justification of the Pyramids, which introduce stern geometry, the completest order, into a landscape. For the same reason, I adored Raphael's *"Sposalizio"* from the moment I first saw it,[6] and for years explored Italy with the hope of finding it realized in these dimensions.

[5] *Vorlesungen über Aesthetik; Einleitung* (Berlin, 1835, 1847) was a posthumous compilation based on notes from his lectures at the University of Berlin.

[6] In *The Central Italian Painters* (1897), B. B. had written of Raphael Sanzio's picture, which was painted for the Franciscans at Città di Castello about 1500 and which now hangs at the Brera, Milan: "The earliest and perhaps loveliest revelation of Raphael's gift we shall find in his 'Sposalizio.' In essentials it is, as a space-composition, but a variant on the fresco of Perugino [Raphael's master] that we studied in the Sixtine Chapel. . . . The elements and the principle remain the same, but the indwelling spirit is not the same. Subtler feeling for space, greater refinement, even a certain daintiness, give this 'Sposalizio' a fragrance, a freshness that are not in Perugino's fresco. In presence of young Sanzio's picture you feel a poignant thrill of transfiguring sensation, as if, on a morning early, the air cool and dustless, you suddenly found yourself in presence of a fairer world, where lovely people were taking part in a gracious ceremony, while beyond them stretched harmonious distances line on line to the horizon's edge."

46

4 APRIL Glanced through *Asiatica*, an imitation of the American *Asia*. The articles seem to have been written by people who know what they were talking about but at a given moment felt a twitch of the thumbscrew, reminding them that the rest of their music must be to the tune of "*Gott strafe England*." Daniele Varé, son of an English mother, naturally is the most anti-British at the end of his slight but otherwise entertaining article on the centenary of Hong Kong. ∼ Getting rather bored with Caroline Schlegel's letters—too often merely domestic.

5 APRIL In Caroline's letters I find now intercalated a number of Friedrich Schlegel's. He seems to have been the naughty boy of the romantic movement,[7] combining in himself Clive Bell, Osbert Sitwell, and even Lytton Strachey, our recent Bloomsbury circle.[8] Only that he and Wilhelm together were enlargers of horizons and conquerors of kingdoms we still are exploring, which is scarcely the case with the above-mentioned Bloomsbury geniuses. Pity there is no good book about either Friedrich or August Wilhelm Schlegel!

[7] Friedrich von Schlegel (1772–1829) was the younger brother of Caroline's first husband, August Wilhelm, with whom he edited the *Athenaeum*, which became the organ of the romantic school. His "naughty boy" period resulted in such experimental works as *Lucinde* (on free love) and his view that the comprehension of life depended on richness and variety of experience. After 1808, when he and his wife (Moses Mendelssohn's daughter Dorothea) became Catholics, his viewpoint was more conservative.

[8] The "Bloomsbury Group" was so called from the London district in which most of its members lived. It flourished from about 1912 and included Virginia and Leonard Woolf, the painter Roger Fry, the novelist E. M. Forster, and the economist J. M. Keynes, in addition to the art critic Clive Bell, the poet and novelist Osbert Sitwell, and the biographer Lytton Strachey. They regarded themselves as devoted to the ruthless "pursuit of truth and a contemplation of beauty . . . in a gentlemanly society."

6 APRIL Finished [Plato's] *Lysis* and began the *Symposium*. Nothing in literature surpasses the charm of the setting of the playful, friendly, highbred yet easy courtesy of tone characterizing all the persons concerned. And in language as natural and simple as Jane Austen at her best. Yes, a great novelist was lost in Plato. Although he has been translated so often, and lends himself so well to translation, it is only in the Greek that his quality as an artist comes out fully.

7 APRIL A tendency in *Osservatore Romano* and in Giovanni Papini's organs to Christianize the Renaissance.[9] It is based on a confusion which it is hard to believe due to ignorance or stupidity only. As a movement, the Renaissance was not Christian and cannot possibly be Christianized. On the other hand as a *period*, the Italian *quattrocento* was overwhelmingly Catholic, even pietistic, and given to revivalism of an almost American-Negro emotionalism. Think of Vincent Ferrer, who was active in Italy as well as in Spain and in the south of France, of San Bernardino, of Giovanni da Capistrano, and of numberless others. A movement of a cultural kind seldom affects even one per cent of a population. I am sure that during the Renaissance few Italians were aware of it as a separate event.

8 APRIL *Die Deutsche Allgemeine Zeitung* rejoices at every sign of England's subordination to America. So did the French press when Austria was losing to Prussia. It took Sedan to make the hereditary enemies of Austria begin to

[9] Papini (1881–1956) had been the editor of literary reviews as early as 1903. In the 1940's, he was associated with *Frontespizio* and was contributing to other reviews and periodicals. His best-known works in America are the *Life of Christ* (1921), written after he had embraced Catholicism at the end of World War I, and *The Devil* (1953).

realize that, by the weakening of Austria, they and not the Austrians might be the greater losers. What advantage would it be to Europe to have England reduced to the condition of a bridgehead between America and the Continent?

9 APRIL The Axis press delights in describing the destruction of Anglo-American shipping by their submarines, and gloats over it. One cannot reproach them; no doubt the other side would do the same. Yet can they be so unforeseeing as not to reflect that when the war is over, no matter who wins or loses, it will be the Continental countries that will suffer most from the lack of bottoms to carry food to them from overseas—food, and every other necessity of our highly organized urban life?

10 APRIL I have often thought that Goethe owed much to his not being afraid of uttering commonplaces, and of being prolix and even dull. A good instance is the slightly facetious dialogue known as *Der Sammler und die Seinigen.*[1] It drags on for some sixty pages, and what little of interest—it is little enough—it contains is found in the last three or four. Despite Goethe's reputation on the matter, art is not his province. Elsewhere this rueful leisureliness in writing can be agreeable and even fruitful, as in *Herrmann und Dorothea,* or even in *Wilhelm Meister.*[2]

11 APRIL Finished Bosanquet and admire the honest effort to state what writers on aesthetics meant, before attempting to criticize them. The result is that one leaves the

[1] Written in 1798–99.
[2] *Herrmann und Dorothea* (1797) is a domestic epic. *Wilhelm Meister's Apprenticeship,* the prototype of the German novel of character development, was begun in 1777 and published in 1796 (Carlyle's English translation in 1824). Its sequel, *Wilhelm Meister's Wanderings,* is a somewhat disconnected series of related short stories published in installments late in Goethe's life (1821–29).

book with some fair sense of what it is all about. My mind refuses to follow [Eduard] von Hartmann and others who labor over the problem of ugliness. To me it seems puerile to regard anything as ugly except in the sense that it is lifeless. Aesthetics seems more filled with problems that don't exist than even other branches of "philosophy," so called.

12 APRIL Finished Voigt with no end of grateful appreciation, and began Burckhardt's *Kultur der Renaissance,* the which also I had not read in fifty years.[3] Very brilliant from the very start, but find some faults as I did then. It subsumes too much time for certain characteristics. What may be true for 1400 is no longer so for 1450 or utterly false for 1500. Yet it is all Renaissance. Startling things recounted in a few pages produce the impression of having taken place continually and everywhere, whereas then, as always, life dragged on in a relatively slow, quiet fashion.

13 APRIL In *Deutsche Biographie,* article on Herder.[4] He seems to have suffered, almost from the moment that Goethe had him called to Weimar, from jealousy, unconsciously perhaps, and taking the shape of disapproving Goethe's paganism, his rather loose living, his indifference, etc., etc. Unfortunately it poisoned Herder more and more,

[3] Jacob Burckhardt (1818–97), Swiss historian, was a student of Ranke. A pioneer in cultural history, he influenced Nietzsche, his friend and fellow professor at Basel. *Die Kultur der Renaissance in Italien* was first published in 1860 (although the Berenson library copy is the 1891 Stuttgart edition); in translation, as *The Civilization of the Renaissance in Italy,* it is now widely known in American academic circles.

[4] Johann Gottfried von Herder (1744–1803), a leader in the *Sturm und Drang* movement, made contributions to philology and to the study of comparative religion and mythology, and developed an evolutionary approach to history. His appointment at Weimar was as court preacher, a post which provided facilities and time for his scholarship from 1776 until his death.

ended by estranging him from Goethe and notably embittering his own life, as well as setting him to write what could not help being tainted with traces of the same unhappy feeling.

14 APRIL Goethe's cry of joy over his discovery of Gothic in the person, as it were, of the Strasbourg cathedral. It speaks well for the youth of twenty-two, brought up strictly in the "*Zopf*" tradition, to feel and vibrate so consciously, so aggressively even, over his discovery.[5] Surprisingly enough he goes to all lengths of nationalism and reaches chauvinism in matters of taste and art history. He glories in the word "Gothic" and hopes it means that the style was really brought in by his Gothic ancestors, to the confusion of the French.

15 APRIL In *Deutsche Biographie*, article on Wilhelm and Alexander von Humboldt. Writer deplores that the first so greatly preferred cultivating himself and satisfying his curiosities to serving the government, although he had great administrative and political qualities.[6] He feels called upon to excuse Alexander's lack of enthusiasm for national causes by the fact that he had lived so long abroad

[5] The "in person" discovery of Gothic at Strasbourg, where Goethe spent 1770–71 completing his law studies, was supplemented by additional discoveries made through his acquaintance there with Herder and other romantics. It was there that he developed his enthusiasm for Germany's medieval past and also for Shakespeare. "*Zopf*" (literally "pigtail") is used figuratively to refer to pedantry and red tape—an allusion here to Goethe's home environment and to his early education, up to the age of sixteen, received at home at the hands of his unbending father, a wealthy Imperial Councilor. His mother was the daughter of Frankfurt's mayor.

[6] The complaint presumably refers to the period after 1819, when Wilhelm von Humboldt (1767–1835) withdrew from the government in opposition to its reactionary spirit. Until then, the philologist and friend of Goethe and Schiller had been one of Prussia's

and got to feel that every nation had its own qualities which were equally valuable—and faults equally deplorable.

16 APRIL In *Osservatore*, a most objective and judicious article on Indian politics such as Italians when disinterested can do as well, at least, as anyone, and perhaps even better. In *Deutsche Allgemeine Zeitung*, a very informative article on Alaska, its resources, and its strategic importance, commanding the air routes of the Pacific, etc. Scarcely a reference to the war except a sentence at end, leaving the Germans free to believe that the Japs will seize it and hold it forever.

17 APRIL Plato's *Symposium*. Good enough, although rather disappointing till Alcibiades reels in with his flute, girls, and Bacchic routs. His drunken discourse is one of the marvels of literature, and the way Plato makes one feel the personages and the atmosphere stamps him as a potential novelist of the highest order, if the novel had existed in his day. His dialogues and trialogues are dramatized talk that is different from Bernard Shaw's only in being less deliberately stagy and totally free from *nouveau riche* impudence and boastfulness in matters of the spirit.

18 APRIL Kant's treatise published in 1764, *On the Sublime and the Beautiful*. Frisky and light, witnessing not only to immense reading on all subjects besides philosophy but to acquaintance with society and with life. He recounts many entertaining anecdotes and *bons mots*, and writes more like a Frenchman than the severe, cold German hard

---

liberal reformers. His role in government had included a term as Prussia's Minister of Education, during which he instituted major reforms. His brother Alexander (1769–1859) was the biologist whose South American and Russian expeditions initiated an era of scientific exploration.

thinker we expect him to be.[7] ~ Caroline's letters, so far as preserved, become really interesting when she falls in love with Schlegel.

19 APRIL When Igor Markewitch dines with us, he reads aloud a translation into French of *Don Quixote*, made directly on publication of original. The language is extraordinarily crisp, sparkling, and picturesque.[8] More contemporary than ever appears the Don, victim at once of an unbridled imagination, of the absence of a sense of reality, and of wishful thinking. These are the very qualities that characterize the geniuses who engaged us in a war that whatever way it goes will not answer their wishes, nor correspond to their dreams and imaginings.

20 APRIL Finished Churchill's *Marlborough*, a great work of art by a great historian. But it sickens one with human nature, and more still with British politics as then practiced. It was then as selfish, as greedy, as violent, as unscrupulous, as ignorant, as improvident as the worst French politics of our day. In that one respect, however, progress cannot be denied. May one hope for a time when the French, too, will learn to play the game, instead of seeing a traitor and a *vendu* in every opponent.

[7] Immanuel Kant (1724–1804): *Beobachtungen über das Gefühl des Schönen und Erhabenen*. The work was written before Kant achieved his professorship at Königsberg—before the period of his great philosophical writings and enormous influence. For a number of years he lectured in various sciences and was acquainted with society through his role as a tutor in wealthy families.

[8] The translation is undoubtedly that of César Oudin, published in Paris in 1614. Oudin, a Frenchman who was a teacher of Spanish, was well acquainted with the Castilian of Cervantes's time. This is, of course, only Part I of *Don Quixote*, since the original publication of Part II did not occur until the following year. François de Rosset was the first translator into French of Part II (1618), and a combined Oudin-Rosset rendering of the full work appeared in 1633; it has remained the standard French version ever since.

21 APRIL Have done well to continue Caroline Schlegel's letters, for with the death of her daughter, and the beginning of her intimacy with Schelling, they not only become excitingly interesting because of this drama but reveal a clearheaded thinker capable of coping with the literature as well as with the philosophy of her day in their greatest width and deepest depth. Full of suave and sound advice given to Schlegel on his relations to others and to Schelling on his relations with herself.

22 APRIL Read about Polybius in Bury's *Greek Historians*. How refreshing to me is Bury's critical mind, interpretative of facts, reasoning from cause to effects, doing its best to arrive at causes. Endlessly more delightful than the metaphysical or merely dialectical one. For similar reasons I enjoy reading the one German of our time with a kindred mind—I mean Eduard Meyer.[9] I can follow all his reasoning step by step and am never plunged as it were into an air pocket.

23 APRIL Finished Bury's *Greek Historians*, which ends with some pages on "Greek" historians writing Latin—e.g., Livy, Tacitus, and before them Sallust—as well as with some remarks on the difference between the historians of antiquity and those of today. Chief difference being our having "historical perspective," although he warns us that future ages may find our standpoint as lacking in the possibilities of depth and breadth and penetration as we find the ancients.

24 APRIL Having finished Churchill's *Marlborough*, we wanted to know what happened with the accession of the Hanoverians. Unfortunately, found nothing readable in

[9] A note on Meyer will be found at February 9.

our own library and took up with J. M. Robertson's *Boling-broke and Walpole*.[1] But Robertson does not narrate at all, and thinking you know the events and the characters, sets out to analyze and interpret them. This he does well enough, and happily with little partisan's Labourite spirit or dogmatism. What a many-sided writer poor J. M. R. was.

2 5 APRIL Plato's *Gorgias*, with the perfectly convincing but not at all persuading plea that the man who does wrong and carries it off and dies unpunished is the most miserable of creatures, for to do wrong is a greater evil than to suffer it, etc., etc. Entertaining dialectics, but one does wish the interlocutors were more like Socrates and better able to hit back. They never are, and fall too easily into his dialectical pitfalls and traps. No wonder he keeps his good humor and great politeness throughout.

26 APRIL Callicles appears at last in the *Gorgias* and stands firmly for his plea that Socrates' talk is nonsense and that the only right is might of the stronger over the weaker. ⁓ In Caroline's letters, the ever stronger impression that she had a pretty art of making enemies. Schlegel's brother Friedrich accused her of deliberately wanting to separate Wilhelm from him, Friedrich, and all other friends. She never misses a chance to carp and sneer at Schiller as man or as artist.

27 APRIL Callicles goes on to tell Socrates that it is time to leave childish things: Philosophy is all right for young people, just as playing with toys is for children; but it is ludicrous in grown-ups, since philosophy does not pre-

[1] London, 1919. John Mackinnon Robertson (1856–1933) was a politician and a humanist writer of literary criticism and unorthodox studies of Christian history.

pare a man for the market or the law court, where he may have to defend his head against rascally accusations. When the late Lord Crawford was young, he and I talked of his Caetani cousins. To clinch what he had to say about them, he burst out with: "Why, the beggars read!" What an accusation!

28 APRIL Callicles talks as an Italian *signore* of the Renaissance would have, could he have expressed himself as clearly. I enjoy the better translations in the Loeb Classics. Besides facilitating the reading of the originals, they offer idiomatic versions that entertain and instruct me as much almost as the text. I am a poor and easily perplexed translator, and feel happy to discover in others the right transposition into English of another language.

29 APRIL Finished Robertson's *Bolingbroke and Walpole*. Later chapters more narrative and descriptive of events and conditions, more interesting than earlier ones discussing matters requiring intimate acquaintance with the events. His picture of Walpole has many points of resemblance with Churchill's *Marlborough*. Being verbal, most of the one could be transferred to the other without disturbing, as would be the case in painting, the actual likeness.

30 APRIL Thackeray's *Four Georges*,[2] superficial, brilliant, full of good sense. Insists that he is not writing political history, but something quite new, social history. On the whole and for the purpose he does it well enough. ～ Began by myself Hervey's memoirs,[3] preceded by a tedious

---

[2] William Makepeace Thackeray (1811–63): *Four Georges* (1860). The work is based on lectures delivered in America in 1855–56.
[3] John, Baron Hervey of Ickworth (1696–1743): *Memoirs of the Reign of George II to the Death of Caroline* (2 vols., London,

life. Hervey is the most unarchaic person I have yet touched of his period, betraying itself only by its constant contrasts. His English at least as good as Voltaire's French. ∼ Reading Caroline's letters I have felt puzzled again and again to know who the principal characters were and just what their relations were to her. The notes did not enlighten me, nor the separate articles in *Deutsche Biographie.* Germans are so eager to understand and to criticize that they cannot easily condescend to begin by giving the facts, by telling what it is all about. That is a blessed gift of the Anglo-Saxons. Almost any English miss will take a subject, get it up and give a plain account which sticks in memory. To return to Caroline: I luckily have received a monograph about her telling me just what I want to know, although it seems to take far too favorable views of her from beginning to end. The author is called Barbara Allason and writes in Italian. I wonder who she is, Scandinavian perhaps rather than English or American.[4]

---

1848). Lord Hervey was a politician and favorite of Queen Caroline. Pope attacked him as "Lord Fanny" and as "familiar toad, half froth, half venom." His bitter memoirs remained unpublished for a century after his death.

[4] Miss Allason, a student of the German romantic school, was born in northwestern Italy in 1877 and lectured on German literature at Turin University for many years. The monograph, written in 1919, was published as *Carolina: Studio sul Romanticismo Tedesco* (Bari, 1939).

## May 1942

| S | M | T | W | T | F | S |
|---|---|---|---|---|---|---|
| 3 | 4 | 5 | 6 | 7 | 1/8 | 2/9 |
| 10 | 11 | 12 | 13 | 14 | 15 | 16 |
| 17 | 18 | 19 | 20 | 21 | 22 | 23 |
| 24/31 | 25 | 26 | 27 | 28 | 29 | 30 |

1 MAY *Gorgias* more and more interesting and contemporary, how the people submit to tyranny, etc. Beautiful the indictment against Pericles, Cimon, and Miltiades for having left the Athenians worse than they found them. ∽ Charmed with Barbara Allason's *Carolina*, written with warmth and affection, giving a most attractive picture of her society. ∽ Thackeray's *Four Georges*. Excellent in a way, but lacking in that framework of political events without which social history does not hang together.

2 MAY Finished *Gorgias*, the most entertaining of all yet read of Plato, and singularly *zeitgemäss* ["seasonable," "timely"] in giving the eternal tooth-and-claw view of society and its infinitely remote opposite, going far beyond anything in the Gospels, not to speak of constitutional Christianity. Socrates' view of sin and expiation nobler as well as more practical. ∽ Also Allason's *Carolina*, whom it rather

58

idealizes, but with persuasiveness, warmth, and charm, portraying her full length as no German hitherto read by me has ever attempted to do.

3 MAY Nicky read aloud in an almost exactly contemporary translation of *Don Quixote* into French. I was struck by great likeness in ejaculation and in every approach to subject with Mardrus's *Mille et une Nuits.*[5] I wonder whether it is due to Mardrus modeling himself on this translation or whether in Cervantes there is a residue of Arab story-telling. If that were so, it would prove how strong an imprint on Spanish letters was left by Arab civilization, fully as much as in the visual arts.

4 MAY As I have occasion to consult a volume of *Deutsche Biographie*, I look at all items of interest. They consist of entries for people known to me not only as names but even as careers and values—they are people, however, about whom I have never read a biographical account. How much one would like to know more about what one cannot give time to. One's ignorance increases as one reads. One finds persons, places, events referred to, whether hitherto unmentioned or too vaguely to satisfy, and one hungers for more till either accident or imperative need drives one to procure information.

5 MAY Don Quixote, whom we are reading, has immunized himself against facts by assuming that when things go against all his expectations, it is the work of enchanters. It is just like the subjects of totalitarian regimes who are so

---

[5] *Le Livre de Mille Nuits et Une Nuit: Traduction littérale et complète du texte Arabe* (16 vols., Paris, 1899–1904). Joseph Charles Mardrus, who made this standard French translation of the *Arabian Nights*, was born in Cairo.

thoroughly indoctrinated against the democracies that nothing coming from the other side can affect them. It is all lying, impudent propaganda. During the last war, English newspapers were freely sold in Berlin; the government rightly believed that no properly conditioned subject would give credence to what he read in a British daily.

6 MAY Got to the literary part of Thackeray's *Four Georges*. Descriptive and anecdotal, but in a dull and perfunctory way. No intellect visible. Criticism confined to contrasting manners and customs of those days with his own, and an occasional sneer at his own. ∽ Perusing the volumes of *Deutsche Biographie*, have been struck by entire absence of anti-Semitism.[6] Jewish items are treated as fairly and considerately as those regarding real Teutons. Makes me doubt whether in Germany there was more reason for anti-Semitic outbreaks than elsewhere in Europe.

7 MAY Finished *Moby Dick*.[7] Unlike my recollections, turns out to be an encyclopedia of South Sea whaling in beautiful, Biblical, Miltonic English. Fine is the opening at New Bedford, and the characters of the South Sea Islands harpooners. Ahab is only a rebel, not a Prometheus but rather like many a hero of Icelandic and early German sagas, or like such a character as Von Bork in Meinhold's *Die Klosterhexe*,[8] capable of bursting asunder out of rage, and

---

[6] *Allgemeine Deutsche Biographie* runs to fifty-six volumes and was published at Leipzig over the years 1875 to 1912.

[7] Herman Melville (1819–91): *Moby Dick* (2 vols., London, 1922). The novel was first published in 1851; this edition dates from the period when Melville began to be rediscovered after a half century of obscurity.

[8] Wilhelm Meinhold (1797–1851): *Sidonia von Bork, die Klosterhexe. . . .* Lady Wilde's English translation, *Sidonia the Sorceress*, was published in London in 1894. The sorceress was the supposed destroyer of the whole ducal house of Pomerania.

of playing the Samson unprovoked. The most beautiful thing in the book is the description of shoals of whales basking in the South Seas.

8 MAY Read Plato's *Menexenus,* a parody of a funeral oration done so discreetly, although so manifestly, that it was taken in earnest at the time and by many still is. It is the ideal of a patriotic speech, and with change of names could prove most handy today. There is no hubristic self-praise it omits, no insistence it does not reiterate on how beautiful it is to die for one's fatherland, and after all how good an investment or life insurance. What fun! It reminds me of Samuel Butler's *Fair Haven.*[9]

9 MAY M. Carrière's article on Börne in *Deutsche Biographie.* I recall how well known Carrière was during my youth.[1] I doubt whether I ever heard of him since. And Börne himself.[2] I wonder whether anyone reads him now excepting, of course, students whose job it is to do so. Who now has the leisure to read him, and still less those who have written about him! Of course, they were as worth reading as

---

[9] Butler (1835–1902) wrote *The Fair Haven* as a satirical defense of the miraculous element in the ministry. It purported to be by "John Pickard Owen," of whom a satirical biography was appended; it was taken seriously by some reviewers. *The Fair Haven* appeared in 1873, and thirty years later Butler, in his only novel, *The Way of All Flesh,* again dealt with Victorian ecclesiastical life, a subject for which he was well prepared since both his father and his grandfather were eminent clergymen.

[1] Moritz Carrière (1817–95) was a German philosopher who taught at Giessen.

[2] Ludwig Börne (1796–1837) was, with Heine, an initiator of the Jewish influence in German literature. In 1818, he became a Protestant convert and changed his name from its original Löb Baruch. He was a brilliant literary critic, but he regarded literature mainly as a weapon in the struggle for political and social advance. His satirical writings opposed censorship and supported a number of liberal movements.

61

most contemporary writing, but they do not talk of what interests us now and here.

10 MAY In volume of *Deutsche Biographie*, published 1893, I found the following in the article on Baron Stockmar: [3] "England with all her healthy and justifiable egotism is free from blind greed, blind envy, and does not try to further her own greatness and prosperity through weakening other states and holding them down." What was said in the 1850's by the men in all the world who best understood England as a great power is ever so much more true in the 1940's. But before the above-mentioned article was published, William, as Crown Prince and then as Emperor, fanned the embers of envy, jealousy, and spite in Germany to her undoing in 1919, and worse is now to follow.

11 MAY In *Laches,* Plato tries to arrive at an understanding of courage. Indescribably charming is the sparring between great gentlemen, on familiar terms with each other, and their unintended, certainly unconscious, condescension toward Socrates. His wits alone might not have won their favor, but they had seen how splendidly he had played his part as a soldier. Where else before the eighteenth century among upper-class Italian, French, and English was there a society of such refinement and elegance as well as simplicity!

12 MAY Barbara Allason's *Bettina*,[4] more interesting, more informing, more convincing than her *Carolina*. Her

[3] Christian Friedrich von Stockmar (1787–1863) was the physican at the Saxe-Coburg court who became friend, traveling companion, and political adviser of both Prince Albert (Queen Victoria's consort) and Leopold (King of the Belgians).
[4] *Bettina Brentano* (Bari, 1927). Bettina von Arnim (1785–1859), the wife of the poet Achim von Arnim, was a member of the cul-

62

*laundry*

*instructors*

*tests*

~~missals~~

*lectionary*

*Confidence in God*

*Book of Canons*

*att Jock Ryan*

*rith Marvea*

Bettina is a demonic creature, sincere and genuine through all her excesses and her seeming absurdities and affectations; she is, as well, a pioneer in seeing and feeling things long before others—a real prophetess, therefore. I wonder, all the same, whether reading her own writings I should get so clear an impression of her as I do through this little book about her. Too often one is disappointed when trying to make contact with what enthusiastic writers have written about.

13 MAY How entertainingly Plato's *Protagoras* begins. The youths panting with eagerness to see Protagoras, waking up Socrates before dawn asking him to come and introduce him. They arrive and have some difficulty in getting admittance. They finally find him walking in cloister, surrounded by devoted admirers, not only from Athens but foreigners who accompany him on his travels. The choreography of how they never allow him to remain behind, but separate off to right and left, going around to come together behind him. Every new dialogue I read makes me regret more and more that the novel was not yet thought of in Plato's day—the novel of humours.

14 MAY Finishing Burckhardt's *Kultur der Renaissance*. I wonder how much he found ready at hand and to what extent he was a pioneer. By pioneer I do not mean one who adventures through the jungle of archives and the des-

---

tivated Brentano family. With her brother Clemens, she was active in the younger romantic circle. In her early years, she was a friend of Beethoven and, supposedly, of Goethe. Her *Goethes Briefwechsel mit einem Kinde* ("Goethe's Correspondence with a Child"; 1835), about which B.B. makes some comments in later Diary entries, has been considered unreliable by some of Goethe's biographers. A characterization of Bettina by Caroline Schlegel is quoted by B.B. in his Diary entry for June 8.

erts of print, but one who is among the first to have certain notions, to make certain guesses, to ask certain questions never clearly made or put before, and to substantiate or abandon his guesses in accordance with the results of his researches. What prodigious reading Burckhardt must have done, and how enviably he marshals his appointed anecdotes and historical facts!

15 MAY Enjoyed Protagoras' lecture on gifts bestowed on individuals and on all in common, first as a parable and then as exposition, amounting to need of accepting the lesser evil, considering evil cannot be gotten rid of. Then Socrates begins his chess game, his quibble, and ends by annoying the old man. Socrates perceives this and prepares to leave. He will not stay if Protagoras will not give short answers to brief questions; he came to discuss and not to hear a lecture or popular harangue. On the whole, Socrates up to this point does not cut the better figure. Protagoras in many ways seems nearer to us in his approach to problems.

16 MAY *"Si ce sonnet n'est guère intelligible, tant mieux, mon Ami. Les sonnets, les odes, et les autres ouvrages qui veulent du sublime ne s'accomodent pas du simple et du naturel; c'est l'obscurité qui en fait tout le mérite, il suffit que le poète croit s'entendre. . . . Nous sommes cinq ou six novateurs hardis qui avons entrepris de changer la langue du blanc au noir; et nous en viendrons à bout s'il plait à Dieu, en dépit de Lope de Vega et de Cervantes."*—Le Sage in *Gil Blas*, quoted by Sainte-Beuve in *Causeries* (II, 368).[5] How

[5] "If this sonnet appears completely unintelligible, my friend, so much the better. Sonnets, odes, and other writings that aim at the sublime cannot be adapted to the ordinary and the natural; in their very obscurity lies their merit, and it is enough that the poet feels himself in accord. . . . We are five or six bold innovators, who have taken it upon ourselves to change the language from white

this parallels the efforts of T. S. Eliot, Joyce, Gertrude Stein, not to speak of others in literature. They will leave even less trace.

17 MAY "Common folk . . . owing to their inability to carry on a familiar conversation over their wine by means of their own voices and discussions—such is their lack of conversation—put a premium on flute-girls by hiring the extraneous voice of the flute at a high price, and carry on their intercourse by means of its utterance. But where the party consists of thorough gentlemen who have had a proper education, you will see neither flute-girls nor dancing-girls, nor harp-girls, but only the company contenting themselves with their own conversation, and none of these fooleries and frolics—each speaking and listening decently in turn. . . ." So Socrates in *Protagoras,* 347 D. So Athens too had its folks who had gramophones beside them, or jazz, or bridge to keep talk away. But in our time the dread of conversation has invaded classes higher than in Athens.

18 MAY Began Huizinga's *Waning of the Middle Ages.*[6] It has the fault of all such writing, no matter how well done, of not insisting enough on the permanent ele-

---

to black; God willing, we will carry it through to the end, in spite of Lope de Vega and Cervantes." The quotation is from *Gil Blas* (1715–35), a famous romance in the Spanish picaresque tradition in which the French novelist and dramatist Alain-René Le Sage (1668–1747) satirized the manners and intellectual life of the time. *Causeries du lundi* ("Monday Chats") is a fifteen-volume collection of the weekly critical articles and reviews written between 1851 and 1862 by Charles Augustin de Sainte-Beuve (1804–69).

[6] Johan Huizinga (1872–1945) was professor of history at the University of Leiden from 1915 until its closing by the Nazis. This work was first published in 1919; since the appearance of an English translation (1924), the work has gained a wide audience in America.

ments in society which change scarcely at all and in which any given moment is but as a bubble. Huizinga will no doubt speak of the Van Eycks as exponents of this period. Far from being melancholy, fantastic, or capricious, they represent calm, serene objectivity as much as the best Greek art, although they lack that art's acquisition of beautiful patterns and shapes.

19 MAY Huizinga on his title page and preface confines his book to the Low Countries and northern France, but as one reads one becomes aware that he seems unacquainted with what went on in the rest of the world. He talks of ceremonial and does not seem to realize that it represents a stage in development. Certain "savages" are intolerably ceremonious, and so are the Japs to this day. He speaks of ceremonial wailing and does not look out and see how much of it has come up from the Near East, where it is still universal, although not in Islam. It takes a very high civilization to get rid of ceremonial except in ritual, as was the case with the Greeks and Hebrews—apparently.

20 MAY In midst of much German criticism and literary history, happened to take up a volume of Sainte-Beuve's *Causeries,* and read it with such relief, such a feeling of happy home-coming. The Germans, even the best, use their thinking machine like an instrument recently discovered, and expensive—one that they love to show off on all occasions, even as small boys their toy autos in a sitting room. They employ it as a dredging machine where a watering can would be in place. They never allow you to forget it. Sainte-Beuve and his peers in France have thought and researched before they sit down to write, and they present their conclusions with restfulness and charm.

21 MAY Mary read aloud *Tom Jones.* Trenchant language, fresh and unconventional, but his desire to show off human nature as it is, to explode humbug, leads him more often than we can enjoy away from presentation to comment, exposition, and interpretation. For his contemporaries no doubt useful, but nowadays, accustomed as we are to the modern novel with its minimum of showman's work, it dates too much. Yet the actual business is of the highest order, far above Hogarth as art.[7]

22 MAY Finished Plato's *Meno.* Interesting when bumping up against the question as to how we know we know, following upon the answer given by a slave boy to a question about geometrical figure. By the way, what a wide-awake and, one would think, educated slave. Suggests that what we recall we recognize as having known in a former existence. ∼ Article on Kleist in *Deutsche Biographie,* amounting to a detailed account. More pathological than I was aware, but tragic and very distressing nevertheless.[8] Singularly disintegrating the effect of Kant upon him.

23 MAY Read Buzzati's *Il Deserto dei Tartari,* suggested no doubt by Kafka, and as dreary almost as Melville's "Bartleby."[9] The story is of a young lieutenant who arrives

[7] Henry Fielding (1707-54): *Tom Jones, a Foundling* (1749). After his plays had provoked the establishment of political censorship in England, Fielding turned to novels as a means of attacking social evils and human faults with savage satire. At much the same time, William Hogarth was pursuing a similar end through his prints.
[8] Heinrich von Kleist (1777-1811) was a German dramatic poet of unusual vigor and great gifts. His personal life, however, was an unhappy and unsuccessful one, ending in suicide.
[9] Milan, 1940. Dino Buzzati (1906-    ) is an Italian journalist and critic, whose fictional works, although highly individual in style, show strong influences of Franz Kafka. The English translation (1952) is called *Tartar Steppe.* Herman Melville's "Bartleby" is a short story (1855) included in *The Piazza Tales.*

at a distant frontier post to which he is appointed. He hates it at sight and asks what he must do to leave it. Instead, something about it hypnotizes him—mystery seems to hang over it for him, as well as the hope of attack from the neighboring enemy. He passes thirty years there and nothing happens until as a sick and dying man he is packed off, just as an enemy is finally placing his guns to bombard the fortress. The allegory is not impressive, but the atmosphere of the place, the people, and their yielding to the tepid resignations of monotony are well rendered.

24 MAY In *Tom Jones,* the lower orders have the *mœurs* of the late lamented *Lazzarone* [porters or messengers] of Naples, certainly no less shifty, greedy, and ingenious. It is a great relief that Fielding does not mythicize "the people" any more than any other class of population, and I wonder whether I am right in perceiving in his procedure no little imitation of Cervantes—not in the characters of the Don or of Sancho, but in the narrative comments and attitude. When Fielding gets to business, he can narrate and let his personages talk with the best.

25 MAY Huizinga speaks of the effect on popular piety of flyleaves with engravings of the Saviour's sufferings, and of the Dance of Death and similar subjects, representing only what could be visually represented. Today we are passing through a similar phase with the cinema, which can popularize only what it can put before the eyes of an audience. The effects are sure to be bad, since what can be shown on the screen is always action, with exaggerated and forced expression, which will inevitably tend to get accepted as a normal way of looking and acting.

26 MAY Alvaro's *Il Mare*.[1] Begins with saying that the women of Calabrian fisherfolk are not good-looking, except for their fine eyes. A fishing village grows into a watering place frequented by neighboring intelligentsia. Arrives first a northern Valkyrie; she and the males snuffle and spy each other, but she ends with a young fishing lad whose beauty and masculinity absorb her as they irresistibly possess women of the Far North. Then a woman from a neighboring farm, a respectable young wife and mother on vacation, but—and this is odd—alone. She too snuffles and is snuffled at. Finally a youth makes a dead set at her for his first conquest. She comes near losing her head, but recognizes in time that for her this is no place—this sea with its seductions, etc., etc.

27 MAY After so much German and German-minded Italian aesthetic and criticism, I feel as if I had reached a heaven of bliss, a spiritual home, in Sainte-Beuve. How he has digested his metaphysical theology, his logic and learning of every kind, and how he presents you the writer, the personage as seen by trained as well as gifted perception, intelligence, and penetration. And with what human sympathy, almost tenderness, with what courteous severity, when he has to find a fault. How remote from German brutality and arrogance, and from the Italian imitations thereof!

28 MAY Finished Plato's *Euthydemus*, a most farcical affair where two Sophists are taken off with all their quib-

---

[1] Corrado Alvaro (*c.* 1885–1955): *Il Mare* (Milan, 1934). An Italian journalist, editor, writer of novels and short stories, Alvaro achieved a fusion between local-color writing (of his native south of Italy) and his sophisticated literary experience.

bling and "smart-aleck" tricks. They remind me of undergraduate talk I heard among clever students at Oxford in
1888, and even more of the Neo-Catholics they were attacking or defending at that remote period. And yet their methods are not so very different from some employed by
Socrates himself when arguing to trip up, or even with
nobler intentions.

29 MAY Paul Shorey's introduction to his edition of
Plato's *Republic* in the Loeb Library.[2] Delighted with his
protests against pedantry and against the irrelevancy of
most textual criticism, but distressed at his constant references to his own previous publications on Plato as if they
outweighed all that had been done before and by others on
same subject. It is an easy illusion to fall into that nobody
else counts in one's own field. One must dissipate such
illusions or become like Strzygowski who was constantly
quoting himself.[3] ∼ More Sainte-Beuve, bless him. What
enchanting drifting downstream it is to read him.

30 MAY Sainte-Beuve is almost as possessed by the
idea that "nature follows art" as I am. Only he has not
reached the phrase. He seldom loses a chance to show how
at a given moment people come on an author, discover themselves in his writings, and model themselves after his characters. He goes so far as to mention Watteau in the same
connection. As an appreciator and historian of ideas he still

[2] Shorey (1857–1934) was professor of Greek at the University of
Chicago and became an internationally recognized authority on
Plato. *What Plato Said* and *Platonism, Ancient and Modern* are
two of his more popular works.
[3] The teachings of Josef Strzygowski, a Viennese professor of art
history, have been sharply attacked by B. B. in his *Aesthetics and
History* (completed 1941, but delayed in publication until 1947 because of the war).

stands at our head, but does not metaphysicize, does not play the psychologer or dialectician, and for that reason is scarcely noticed by Croce and others like him.

31 MAY Last two numbers of Croce's *Critica*.[4] Whole tone too sectarian, reminding one of the arrogant and overbearing way provincial Roman Catholic prelates attempted to confute Darwin. Pity Croce is so much of an *archisynagogos*, and not only dogmatic to a degree but so prone, almost eager, to bark back at the puppies who venture to yelp at his heels. But what energy, to produce, every two months, articles on technically philosophical as well as on succinct literary erudition, besides reviews. Always Vico and De Sanctis to the fore.[5] Vico, undoubtedly, deserves it, but as for the other, his importance so far as I can make out is local. I cannot recall that he enounced principles or in criticism used methods not already in use. There is, in fact, no little nationalism in Croce, and behind that, sheer professional vanity. I like him best when he is frankly Neapolitan and anecdotic. His sense of human relations is admirable; it is at the bottom of all that is best in his criticism of poetry.

[4] *La Critica*, a "review of literature, history, and philosophy," was edited by Benedetto Croce for nearly half a century. It was published bimonthly at Naples from 1903 to 1944, and quarterly at Bari from 1945 to 1950.
[5] On Giambattista Vico, see the note under February 13. Francesco De Sanctis (1817–83) was a critic and literary historian; his principal work is *Storia della Letteratura Italiana* (1872). He attempted to combine two principles: the idea that a work of art should be looked at by itself as an intuitive product of the human mind, and the idea that it is a document in the spiritual history of a nation.

| June 1942 | | | | | | |
|---|---|---|---|---|---|---|
| S | M | T | W | T | F | S |
| | 1 | 2 | 3 | 4 | 5 | 6 |
| 7 | 8 | 9 | 10 | 11 | 12 | 13 |
| 14 | 15 | 16 | 17 | 18 | 19 | 20 |
| 21/28 | 22/29 | 23/30 | 24 | 25 | 26 | 27 |

1 JUNE My eye falling on the name of Gottsched in *Deutsche Biographie*, and not having had him in mind for many decades, I read the article. He was the critic and man of letters Germany happened to need when he was thirty. By the time he was fifty, it had outgrown him.[6] Of course it repaid him by jeers, sneers, kicks, and buffets for having enabled it to get beyond him, ignoring all it had learned from him, and ignoring even that great part of his teaching which had permanent value. His fate was only to an unusual degree the fate of all of us who have something to say that gets a hearing for a while, only to become a jeering-post sooner perhaps than desirable for the community.

2 JUNE In Plato's *Republic*, Thrasymachus defines justice as that which is advantageous to the ruling class or

[6] Johann Christoph Gottsched (1700–66) was professor of poetry at the University of Leipzig. He upheld the classical tradition of Boileau and Corneille in opposition to that of Shakespeare and the contemporary German lyric poets.

ruler—whether one man, oligarchy, or democracy. All Machiavelli is therein, and it is still the only notion of justice most politicians and most people practice. Even now, when they speak of "peace with justice," they mean justice as it is to their advantage, and without justice if not to their advantage. Furthermore, by advantage they mean immediate and not long-range advantage. How much European, and more especially Mediterranean and German and French, policy of the last decades is explained, or rather actuated, by these notions of advantage and of justice.

3 JUNE Article on Carossa in Alessandro Pellegrini's *Novecento Tedesco.*[7] Quotes him as saying: "Years of reconstruction after ruinous disasters are years favorable to the increase of a people. Only active-minded and reflecting spirits recognize the advantages of defeat, and while others enjoy, muse, curse, whisper, and decree how mankind must henceforward behave, these, few as they are, silently prepare the future." In Poincaré's era, after the last war, hearing of all the follies, not to speak of the crimes, committed by the French, I used to go about muttering *"Vae victoribus, gloria victis."* I was confident that terrible disasters would overtake France before a score of years was over, although I little foresaw the exact shape of the thing.

4 JUNE Caroline's letters decidedly more and more interesting, self-revealing, and informing after she leaves Jena and marries Schelling. What a world the professional and literary one was in Germany at that time. Jealousy, envy, spite, constant conspiring, calumniating, and spiting.

---

[7] Alessandro Pellegrini (1897–    ): *Il Novecento Tedesco* (Milan, 1942). The author, professor of German literature at Milan University, is quoting Hans Carossa (1878–    ), German physician, poet, and autobiographical novelist.

A trick now happily extinct but then current was foul personal attacks, either in the so-called literary journals or in out-and-out anonymous and libelous attacks as flyleaves or pamphlets. No wonder such a people had sooner or later to submit to a severe discipline to learn any kind of team-work.

5 JUNE Proceeding with *Tom Jones*. A contemporary of ours would have made a shortish novel out of it. Fielding elongates it tiresomely (for us) with discourses, boringly with over-spun-out episodes like that of Mrs. Fitz-Patrick, and with his mock-Homeric similes. Everywhere one feels the influence of Cervantes, and perhaps of Le Sage. But what *"mœurs,"* how revoltingly different from those of the France of the same day! Yet highly civilized compared with Germany as the *Bayreutherin,* sister of Frederick the Great, describes it.[8] Think of the provincial gentry she encounters on the way to Bayreuth, and the father-in-law with his court that she finds there!

6 JUNE Finished Huizinga's *Waning of the Middle Ages.* Has a good deal to say about visual art, calls it a period of visual rather than verbal art, because, forsooth, the visual production of that time still surviving interests us today so much more than the verbal. What is so, then? Did the public not take them as one with their costuming, and value the artists much more than their tailors, while they continued to admire equally skilled writers, as in a sense we

[8] The *Bayreutherin* was Wilhelmina (1709-58), the daughter of Frederick William I, King of Prussia. She became Margravine of Bayreuth in 1731. Like her brother, she was highly talented and did considerable writing. Although the accuracy of some details in her travel diaries has been questioned, they provide useful pictures of the period.

74

still do if they attain any quality, despite their present-day ephemerality?

7 JUNE Chamberlin's *Japan over Asia,*[9] informing, suggestive, depressing. I have thought of what would happen if China got militarized, yet failed to reflect that it might become industrialized, using cheaper labor than the rest of the world, including even Japan, whom it could undersell. Whatever happens as the result of the present war, the Far East is lost to us Europeans, and the Middle East will not remain dependent long on our industries. The countries of the Europe-America world will have to get on by taking in each other's washing, and turn their energies to the qualitative, to the internal, rather than to quantitative and extroverted matters.

8 JUNE If all Caroline Schlegel's letters were like the one of March 1, 1809, she could rank along with the best in the epistolary art. In this particular one, she writes of Tiecks and Brentanos, characterizing Bettina unsurpassingly.[1] Here are some sentences: "An odd little mite, physically clinging and yielding, inwardly intelligent but on the outside foolish, decent yet beyond all decorum. Nothing she is or does is pure nature, but at the same time she cannot be anything but what she is. She suffers from the trouble with all Brentanos: an affectation that replaces nature. . . . She is to be found under rather than on the table, and never on a chair. Neither young nor old, neither handsome nor ugly, neither male nor female."

[9] Boston, 1937. William Henry Chamberlin (1897–    ) was for many years foreign correspondent for the *Christian Science Monitor*. Since 1940, he has done independent writing on history and and international politics, and has lectured at Haverford, Yale, and Harvard.
[1] See the note under May 12 and the Diary entry for June 19.

75

9 JUNE Josef Körner's *"Botschaft der Romantik,"* [2] an elaborate account of Schlegel's *Dramaturgische Vorlesungen*—what were its sources, how it was composed, what is good, and what is fluff and hasty. Chief source as always his far more gifted brother, Friedrich. Astounding its universal influence. Translated into French, it went everywhere and carried along such important writers as Pushkin in Russia, Edgar Allan Poe in America, and above all Coleridge, who follows Schlegel so closely that he almost plagiarizes him. A mediocre and for that very reason effective work, coming at the moment when Europe was ready for such an account of the drama.

10 JUNE Finished H. Knittermeyer's *Schelling und die romantische Schule,* [3] of which as philosophy I have understood little, but it has told me much I wanted to know about the relations of Fichte, Hegel, Schelling, Novalis, the Schlegels to one another, and it has roused my curiosity in their contemporaries, Baader,[4] Solger,[5] and Steffens.[6] As for

[2] *"Die Botschaft der deutschen Romantik an Europa"* (1929) appears in Volume IX of *Schriften zur deutschen Literatur der Görres-Gesellschaft.* Körner, professor of German literature at Augsburg, was born in 1888 and died in the 1930's. A. W. Schlegel's *Dramaturgische Vorlesungen* was published in 1809; its English translation, *Lectures on Dramatic Art and Literature,* appeared in 1815. While some of Schlegel's translations (Shakespeare, Dante, Cervantes, Calderón, Camoens) are still considered to have great literary quality, his original writings, despite their extraordinary influence at the time, are now seldom read.

[3] Munich, 1929. Hinrich Knittermeyer (1891– ) is a theologian and philosopher who has been head of the Bremen Library.

[4] Franz Xavier von Baader (1765–1841) was a philosopher and mystic and one of the foremost modern Catholic theologians.

[5] Karl Wilhelm Ferdinand Solger (1780–1819) wrote on philosophy and aesthetics.

[6] Henrik Steffens (1773–1845), German philosopher of Norwegian extraction, taught physics at Breslau and Berlin. He was a friend and adherent of Schelling and Schleiermacher.

the philosophy, my mind cannot penetrate it. I am inclined
to believe that it has no more real foundation than astrology
or alchemy, or the still current chiromancy, not to speak of
the now defunct phrenology. On the other hand, I grant it
is endlessly more stimulating, for which reason I cannot
resist nibbling at it.

11 JUNE Reading Plato—just now the *Republic*,
Book II—I am amazed to discover how well the interlocutors know their poets by heart—not only Homer, but
Pindar, Aeschylus, Simonides, as well. In what way did they
acquire this knowledge, I wonder. Homer, no doubt, was
drummed into them at school, as indeed most of the Old
Testament in Hebrew, and the prayer book, was drummed
into me before I was ten. But I had the text before me. Did
every free Athenian possess his great poets in manuscript?
He knew them so well that he recognized a quotation
quickly, if not immediately. Printing seems to have served
to inform rather than to educate.

12 JUNE Book III, paragraphs 401 and 402 of Plato's
*Republic* give pretty much all I have tried to say about
illustration in the arts: "Is it, then, only the poets that we
must supervise and compel to embody in their poems the
semblance of the good character or else not write poetry
among us, or must we keep watch over the other craftsmen,
and forbid them to represent the evil disposition, the licen-
tious, the illiberal, the graceless, either in the likeness of
living creatures or in buildings or in any other product of
their art, on penalty, if unable to obey, of being forbidden
to practice their art among us, that our guardians may not
be bred among symbols of evil, as it were in a pasturage of
poisonous herbs, lest grazing freely and cropping from

77

many such day by day they little by little and all unawares accumulate and build up a huge mass of evil in their own souls. . . ."

13 JUNE Read in *Republic* of Misologoi, who hated discussion and prefer to get results by out-and-out violence. There we have Fascists and so-called democrats—most unfortunate terms. What is opposed to violent means is not democracy but free discussion, which is to say parliamentary rule. It has its faults like everything human, but in a world where we must look for no more than the least evil, parliamentarism with all its drawbacks is the only possible government for free men, and in the long run for all men. Unhappily, their education to enjoy such a regime is scarcely begun. It should be furthered without delay.

14 JUNE In Bologna or Rome, Erasmus might have known Raphael and Michelangelo, in Venice the old Giovanni Bellini, the fascinating Giorgione, the grandly promising Titian. Blind seemed this northern humanist to art of any kind. How different from his Italian contemporaries, who were so keenly aware of their existence, and their doing. What would one not give for an appreciation of Italian genius in the fine arts by such a sensitive soul as Erasmus. Bad luck that scarcely any letters have reached us from the years he spent in Italy.[7]

[7] B. B. appears to have been reading at this point Johan Huizinga's *Erasmus* in a German translation (Basel, 1928) from the original Dutch edition of 1924. The Dutch scholar-priest's opportunities for exposure to the Italian artists would have come through his visit to Bologna in 1506 as a tutor-companion, his stay in Venice the following year during the preparation of the 1508 expanded edition of his *Adagia*, and his visit to Rome about 1508 as tutor to Alexander Stuart, the natural son of James IV of Scotland.

15 JUNE Bettina writes to Goethe that Tieck, the sculptor,[8] was doing the bust of Schelling. He wanted to elongate the face to make it look more elegant, but the subject insisted on its being as square as possible so as to express the energy he felt full of. So it is with every portrait. The artist has his idea, the subject another, and the latter's relations and friends still others. The result seldom at the time satisfies. If it has real art value, however, it survives, regardless of how like it was to the various views entertained of the subject.

16 JUNE Finished Alessandro Pellegrini's *Novecento Tedesco*, treating of Carossa, Hofmannsthal, Rilke, [Rudolf] Kassner, and Stefan George. Seems to exaggerate Kassner's importance, and to philosophize these writers far too much. Follows account of recent German philosophy outright, from which I make little sense, no doubt owing to my own congenital incapacity and lack of training to be able to cope with such subjects—which, by the way, seem so frivolous to me as to be superfluous. I dare say the fascination comes from their metaphysical problems being eternally insoluble and yet fit to engage the acutest and ablest minds.

17 JUNE Reading Bettina's letters, it occurs to me that there are few writers, excepting the truly great ones of the past, whom I had not rather read about than read themselves. A student like the Allason has lived herself into Bettina as into Caroline; she has sucked all the honey that was in them, and has presented it to us on a silver dish. Reading themselves one has to shell and then to cook, after throwing

---

[8] On the Bettina-Goethe correspondence, see the note under May 12. The Tieck referred to here is Christian Friedrich Tieck (1776–1851), now remembered mainly for his mythological reliefs in the Royal Theater, Berlin.

79

away so much. All this is truer still of most writers of the Middle Ages, and even of the Renaissance. I confess I no longer can stand their "*longueurs*."

18 JUNE In *Japan over Asia*, Chamberlin tries to give an idea of Japanese regime, and speaks of the cult of the Emperor and of the distribution of authority as something peculiar and hard to parallel. But a parallel is not far away, in Great Britain, particularly under Baldwin, Simon, and the Chamberlains. There too power rested in the elder statesmen, in the City, in the servants; and the King—that is, the Crown—is no mere figurehead. To the great majority of the British people everywhere, he is hedged round by a numinism without which the Crown could not be strong enough to hold together all the Dominions without any other tie whatever.

19 JUNE Startled to come across a sentence in Bettina's letters almost implying that she believed she was Goethe's daughter, not after the spirit only but after the flesh. What an example of wishful thinking! How she would have preferred that to being the daughter of a gross, perhaps brutal, entirely worldly Italian grocer from Como! Yet the combination of this grocer with a German gentlewoman produced not only Bettina and Clemens but in later generations Lujo and Franz Brentano, each in his way so distinguished.[9] Half Italian, I learn, was [Joseph von] Görres, and nowadays there are or have been wholly Germanized Italians, [Ferruccio Benvenuto] Busoni and [Romano] Guardini.

[9] Bettina's nephew, Lujo (1844–1931), was a noted political economist; Franz (1838–1917) was a philosopher who helped to establish psychology as a separate science. In the present generation, Brentanos continue to be outstanding: Heinrich, for example, has served as West Germany's Foreign Minister.

20 JUNE Power and authority of the squire, as revealed in *Tom Jones*, scarcely less than that of the petty sovereigns, the *Landesväter*, in Germany. Amazing how dependent everybody in their own parish is on them, and with what cringing awe they are regarded by the lower orders. And yet out of that came the England of our time, where the humblest member of society is more free than he is anywhere on earth, except possibly in the U.S.A. The intimate history of the change must have been written, but I fear in abstract economic, not in human, terms.

21 JUNE Reading into Kant, I am surprised to discover how wise, how deep, but also how witty, he could be. Reading about him, I learn that he was quite a man of the world. His portrait at forty is of an open countenance, not scholastic, but well bred, amiable. And what a liberal he was, and how much more in harmony with my state of mind than most philosophers. Nor is his style so unpolished as expected. Not to that, but to his thought, are due the difficulties of understanding him. He requires concentrated attention for long stretches.

22 JUNE Huizinga concludes that Erasmus is not a great man compared with Luther or Calvin, who are. It occurs to ask what Huizinga and the rest of us mean by a "great man." Presumably it is someone who, being all of a piece, has pushed through, pulled off, or put over through sheer force, whether the result be good or bad. *"Cosa fatta capo ha,"* in short.[1] This kind of person we heroize, we mythicize, we make the subject of song or story; and it ends by having as little relation to what he actually was as the grown-up man has to his own embryo.

[1] "What's done is done."

81

23 JUNE I wonder why the Nazis do not, in their teaching and propaganda, appeal to Plato's *Republic*, where a totalitarian state is pictured that could easily be twisted into being identical with the Nazi attempt—*toute proportion gardée.*[2] Or is it my ignorance of what goes on in Naziland that makes me wonder? The resemblances are certainly startling, but so they are with almost any utopia founded on the static ideal of all-wise rulers and obediently docile ruled. Perhaps nobody more than the Jesuits has approached the Platonic "guardians" in action and in their relation to their own brethren.

24 JUNE One gets the impression that after his sixtieth year Goethe could be gloomy and harsh. For years he would not be reconciled to Bettina, and when in 1821 she forced her way into his presence it led to no satisfactory result. She thereupon writes to him in a way that reveals and explains her attitude toward him as well as her own character. She is a red-hot mystic as much as Saint Catherine, only that the sensuous but not sexual object of her longing is Goethe instead of the Saviour. Viewed in that light, her behavior, her outpourings, her vocabulary grow intelligible and plausible.

25 JUNE Finished Huizinga's *Erasmus*, a good, descriptive book, but he admires Erasmus rather than loves him. One feels that he has failed to really penetrate and to relive the life of his subject, and to make us live it over again, the way the great biographer does. ∼ Finished also Bettina's real letters to Goethe. Once, late in life, he wrote a short note to his sovereign about Bettina of such a brutality that one wonders whether Goethe was a gentleman. He might

[2] "Due allowance being made."

have written that way to one who loved her, not to a reigning prince who had just seen her for the first time!

26 JUNE Plato, in *Theaetetus* (150–151), lets Socrates say: "Many thinking that they are themselves the cause of their success, but despising me, have gone away from me sooner than they ought, whether of their own accord, or because others persuaded them to do so. Then, after they have gone away, they have miscarried . . . and the offspring which they had brought forth with my assistance they have guarded so badly that they have lost it; they have considered mere shows and images of more importance than the truth, and at last it was evident to themselves as to others that they were ignorant. . . . When such men come back and beg me as they do, with wonderful eagerness, to let them join me again . . . , the spiritual monitor that comes to me forbids me to associate with some of them." Thus Socrates not only anticipated my thought for the most part, but some of my experiences as well.

27 JUNE Bettina's connection with Goethe is interesting as a study in the relation of author to his subject matter. In her *Briefe* she has assimilated and wishfully mythicized the material to a degree that satisfied her sense of self and her cult of Goethe. In the letters of each day there is already a transmutation, but with time this grows into mythopoetry. But all *Dichtung* is of that nature, although not so extravagantly as in Bettina, who not only was guilty of wishful thinking as few others have been but was also guilty as almost nobody else of wishful living—that is to say, of experiencing subjectively what she ardently desired.

28 JUNE Friedrich Schlegel's *Lucinde*—fascinatingly keen, zestful, bold, luminous, and impressive.[3] Inspired,

[3] See Note 7 under April 5.

no doubt, by Ossian and Heinse, as well as by Goethe. Singular how small works, written almost contemporaneously, and no doubt independently of each other, like Schlegel's *Lucinde*, Chateaubriand's *René*, and the somewhat later *Adolphe* of Benjamin Constant, should have so much the same mental attitude, the same emotional tone. An instance of "iso-psychology," if ever. Would be interesting to expatiate over this, unless indeed it has been done already.

29 JUNE In Schleiermacher's defense of Friedrich Schlegel's *Lucinde*,[4] he accuses a correspondent of being a prude and advises her to take the first conveyance to England, where ladies will not use the words "chaste" or "decent" because they might suggest the opposite. When did English prudery begin? No trace of it in Fielding or Goldsmith. It must have crept in during the last quarter of the eighteenth century, found a suitable climate, and put forth its utmost as late as my youth, when in U.S.A. people would not pronounce the word "leg," but said "limb"—"limb of a piano." Then some twenty or more years ago, came the complete change, from ignoring everything animal in us to chattering of almost nothing else except sex and the other animal functions.

30 JUNE Finished first volume of Fielding's *Amelia*.[5] Lacks the sparkle and the vitality of a *Tom Jones*, and despite too many episodes in the latter, its unity, its near inevitability. The historical interest of *Amelia* is considerable, as a picture of an England, brutal, cruel, formal, overwhelmingly inhuman—like the worst pictures one had of Neapolitan or Calabrian life not so long ago. Who can deny progress

---

[4] Friedrich D. E. Schleiermacher: *Vertraute briefe über die "Lucinde"* (Berlin, 1800).
[5] Two volumes, London, 1752.

in humanization when one compares the pitiful enough England of our time with that of less than two centuries ago?
∼ It may be deplorable, but I read ever so much more about
the great writers and their works than I read the works
themselves. It is not only because many of them are too
archaic in both language and thought to be enjoyed in the
raw, rather than as premasticated or prepared by critics who
have extracted and tabloided them; it is also because I am
more and more interested in what others have thought and
said about them in the course of the ages. Furthermore, I am
envious to know what expositors who have devoted lives to
understanding this or that great author have to say about
him, and to have them draw my attention to points that
have escaped me. I shall, for instance, never forget the explanation of certain Chinese verses given by Yoshio Markino
in his *When I Was a Child.*[6] It seemed as if he had revealed a
treasure of which hitherto I had seen only the casket that
contained it. Not satisfied with the commentators, I gladly
read *commentators on commentators,* just as now.

[6] London, 1912. Markino (1874–    ), a modern Japanese painter
and book illustrator, is also the author of *A Japanese Artist in
London.*

```
          July 1942
  S  M  T  W  T  F  S
              1  2  3  4
  5  6  7  8  9  10 11
  12 13 14 15 16 17 18
  19/26 20/27 21/28 22/29 23/30 24/31 25
```

1 JULY I have read Santoli's long and learned essay prefixed to his translation of Friedrich Schlegel's *Epigramme*.[7] Not good enough—I mean the Epigrams. It is another matter with Goethe, who interests me as much if not more as a man of letters and as a mere man than as a great writer. The great writers I read as little as I read Shakespeare. Another about whom I never tire reading is Voltaire, and for the same reason—the personage and the man of letters can fascinate one to the extent that one's curiosity gets the better of the desire to read his masterpieces.

2 JULY Ruskin's *Queen of the Air*, eloquent, magniloquent, unctuous, mad, absurd, penetrating, visionary,

[7] *Frammenti Critici e Scritti di Estetica* (Florence, 1937), translated from *Fragmente und Ideen: Kritische Fragmente* (1797–1801) by Vittorio Santoli (1901–    ), professor of German literature at the University of Florence.

fantastic, all in one.[8] What a curious mythopoet is Ruskin, how conveniently he handles the Greek deities with the freedom of old friends whose secret histories he alone knows. "Almost thou persuadest me" to prefer your interpretations to any of the anthropological ones, so laboriously put together by Frazer and his precursors and followers. Yet what sublime impudence on the part of Ruskin.

3 JULY G. K. Chesterton's *Victorian Age in Literature.* A brilliant buffoon, many happy sayings, many quite just, but all on an ocean of unavowed Catholic or Catholicizing medievalism.[9] It is from such a point of view only that Victorian England can be regarded as provincial. Does fair justice to Matthew Arnold as prose-writer, but does not mention his verse, which seems to me to have more permanent value than Tennyson's brainless jingle, or Browning's quasi-Arab ejaculations. Surprising that such an attitude toward the nineteenth century should have been published in the Home University Library!

4 JULY Wölfflin's three short essays on Jacob Burckhardt, interesting information and right in feeling.[1] Burckhardt was one of the greatest humanists of all time and the last effective German one. Reading his *Weltgeschichtliche*

---

[8] London, 1869. The subject matter is the group of Greek myths of cloud and storm.

[9] London, 1929. The original publication occurred in 1913, nine years before Chesterton (1874–1936) became a member of the Roman Catholic Church; much of his earlier work, like this study, already indicated an interest in Catholicism.

[1] In *Gedanken zur Kunstgeschichte* (Basel, 1941). B. B. elsewhere described Heinrich Wölfflin (1864–1945) as "the most disinterested and most constructive of surviving workers on art history," and he went on to say, "Let me take the occasion to declare my own indebtedness to his two books on classical and baroque art [*Die klassische Kunst* and *Renaissance und Barock*]."

*Betrachtungen,*[2] I was amazed in discovering how much he anticipated me in my conclusions regarding the past. How well informed he is and of what sound judgment. Everything he says about Islam, for instance, is masterly and should put to shame the admirers of its civilizations and culture and the believers in its equivalence or even superiority to ours.

5 JULY Leskov's *Sheramur.*[3] I seem unable to understand Russian humor, whether Gogol or Dostoevski or Leskov. If Sheramur were the simple glutton who wanted to loaf through life caring for nothing but quantities of food! But perhaps he is an allegorical figure denoting that the greatest majority of mankind devotes its attention almost entirely to obtaining abundant nourishment for itself, but as a condiment feeding others, and ready to forgo every other ambition for that. How different from Melville's Bartleby, whom nevertheless this character vaguely suggests.

6 JULY Never read pages more interesting, characterizations more apt, history more succinct than in Burckhardt on Church and State in general and the Catholic Church in particular.[4] Masterly in epithets. Speaks of *"Verjunkerung"* of the Church, and nothing could be more true. After conquests had stopped careers for younger sons of feudal nobility, they fell like ravens on the Church and

---

[2] Berlin, 1905 (originally published in 1873). The English translation has appeared as *Force and Freedom: Reflections on History* (1943).

[3] Nikolai Leskov (1831–95): *Sheramur* (Lanciano, 1927). Leskov is the Russian novelist whose *Sealed Angel* contains some most understanding comments on the painter's art.

[4] The essay "On Church and State" is included in *Weltgeschichtliche Betrachtungen.*

pushed at her and picked her and fed on her bile—the French Revolution almost—although the abolition in the seventeenth century of commendam narrowed them down not a little. Burckhardt says much else of the kind, most stimulating.

7 J U L Y Finished Plato's *Sophist*—entertaining definitions splitting every concept into two, and again into two, *ad nauseam* if not *ad infinitum*. To me, of special personal interest is the definition that thinking is talking, conversing with oneself. I did that as early as my fifth year, and before I was six knew that that was thinking. I trust I do not flatter myself by believing that during my "metaphysical age"— my seventh and eighth years—I came very near to the notion of "ideas" in the Platonic sense, as entities absolute and as eternal models of our fluctuating and endlessly varied perceptions.

8 J U L Y Began Plato's *Politicus*, and met with the statement that the King, the master, the boss, and the householder all had the same job, namely housekeeping—a favorite thesis of mine for a long time. It is the opposite of setting up the State as something sacred, august, to which every man and every thing should be subjected. I wonder though whether Plato will carry this through or abandon it for the "idea," which then would result in something identical with the German notion of "*Staat.*"

9 J U L Y In Fielding's *Amelia*, the heroine is at Ranelagh with Dr. Harrison, a young clergyman, and her children. Two dandies, one of them a lord, attempt to make free with her in a way that nowadays seems inconceivable. Even more inconceivable is that the bystanders did not gather others and handle them in a way that would cure

them of such conduct once for all. No, bad as manners still are today, they are endlessly more human than those described by Fielding. In that respect we have made great progress.

10 JULY In *Weltgeschichtliche Betrachtungen*, Burckhardt on great men—admirable as all he ever says on historical subjects, but he does not come near enough to my own formula to state it, namely that what makes them spontaneously and almost universally canonized as great is that they really were irresistibly life-enhancing or that at least they lent themselves to mythicizing propaganda in their own lifetime or in that of their heirs.

11 JULY Finished Burckhardt's suggestive and stimulating *Betrachtungen*, ending with discussion of events leading up to 1870, etc. ∼ Plato in *Statesman* [*Politicus*] speaks of dream knowledge. How well I know this state of mind! He recounts a myth about the gods getting tired, from time to time, of running the world. They let it go its own way, forgetting all about it until the horrors of misgovernment scream to heaven, when in pity they again take the management into their own hands, and things slowly but steadily improve. Let us hope they soon will turn to us and save us!

12 JULY Friedrich Schlegel on poetry in general and Goethe in particular.[5] The general is prettily said, but of no great interest now, although important in its day, insisting on right judgment based on right feeling. As to Goethe, Friedrich Schlegel does little but point to the best poems,

[5] *Gespräche über die Poesie* (1800).

canonizing those we still think the best. More to say about
*Wilhelm Meister* as a pilgrim's progress to culture.[6] He
does not fail to see its weaknesses, but does not dwell on
them. Defends it against the aspersions and misunderstandings of contemporaries.

13 J U L Y In *Forschungen und Fortschritte*, article by
Max Wundt.[7] Seeing that human stocks never change in
character, how is it that a nation does? Answer: A nation is
composed of different stocks, and one or the other of these
is always to the fore and imposes its own character. This
startling discovery has been known to me for forty years at
least. I have been in the habit of attributing "decline" in
culture to the disappearance of its carriers and to their being
replaced by others who, unacquainted with former standards
and tastes, are from our point of view inferior, because less
humanized.

14 J U L Y Gogol's letters, very disappointing except
one to Joukowsky on his literary testament. No wonder he
roused the indignation of the Russian literary folk. They
were all ultraliberal, and the shock must have been great
to discover that one of the most gifted among them had
turned completely away from illuministic liberalism toward
everything that was nationally, Byzantinishly, medie-

---

[6] On *Wilhelm Meister*, see Note 2 under April 10.
[7] Two years later, B. B. was to write: "Have been perusing recent
issues of *Forschungen und Fortschritte*, a German periodical that
kept one up to date in all fields of scholarship, exact science, and
philosophy. It has become more and more imbued with the intellectual perversity of the Nazis." This contributor, Max Wundt
(1879–    ), taught at several German universities. He was the son
of the noted Wilhelm Max Wundt, who established at Leipzig the
world's first laboratory for experimental psychology and who also
was the founder of the science of folk psychology.

vally Russian.[8] In the intellectual and spiritual sense, the Russians were the first nationalists in Europe.

15 JULY What makes Wackenroder[9] interesting is that he did not regard the work of art as something to admire and enjoy on an amateur basis, or as a matter of taste, but as something to feel and live. He was the precursor of Chateaubriand and all who take the Catholic and medieval Church more aesthetically than theologically. How the German romantics anticipate not only Chateaubriand, but Byron, and Wordsworth, and Shelley, and even Keats. Hence too the facility of action and reaction between them, as they became known to each other. I omitted mention of Coleridge only through sheer inadvertence, of course.

16 JULY Finishing Fielding's *Amelia,* I cannot help seeing a close relation between public (political) and private morals and customs. After all, where Mrs. Masham, Queen Anne, Harley, and St. John [Lord Bolingbroke] could flourish in high life, what is one to expect of the people in humbler conditions who certainly were not more heedless, more blackguardly, more inconsiderate of others, nor more given to plotting and backbiting. Surely public morality cannot help influencing general conduct as well as political conduct.

[8] Nikolai Gogol (1809–52): *Lettres sur l'Art, la Philosophie, et la Religion* (Paris, 1926). Gogol experienced a turnabout in his social and political viewpoints as the result of a personal moral and religious crisis. *Dead Souls,* his long novel of violent social satire, indicts serfdom, but his later attitude prevented completion of a projected second part. His correspondent, in the letter discussed above, was the poet Vasili Joukowsky (1783–1852), who, as tutor to Alexander II, suggested the idea of liberating the serfs.
[9] Wilhelm Heinrich Wackenroder (1773–98): *Herzensergiessungen eines kunstliebenden Klosterbruders* (1797). Wackenroder, a poet, had a religious and mystical conception of art that influenced his fellow Jena romanticists.

17 JULY Plato's *Philebus*—scarcely a trace of a doxology or an "Amen." At one point it reaches the very brink of discovering the subconscious. Elsewhere interesting views on art. Curious insistence that music is the least pure of the arts, depending most on experimenting (guessing), whereas to us, in our day, it seems the most mathematical, and certainly the purest—indeed, the quintessence of art. Plato despises an art based not on theory but on mere practice, on mere floundering to and fro; an art that has no canon or has lost it is no art at all, but mere handicraft, etc., etc.

18 JULY In *Lucinde*, Friedrich Schlegel says the privilege of idleness is what everywhere under the sun marks off the aristocrat from the commoner, and is indeed the very essence of nobility. Before the last war, Ugo Ojetti published in the *Corriere della Sera* an article to that effect.[1] The latter's intention was farcically ironical. There is nevertheless a truth in Schlegel's remark, besides the justification of his own idleness. The overworked, driven person or class is seldom creative, while leisure, even wasteful leisure, may end creatively.

19 JULY Read Plato's *Ion*. Exceedingly unfair, for what Ion is driving at but seems too flustered to say, or perhaps too stupid to see, is that the business of the critic in literature is to interpret it as human nature in general, as the man behind the profession, the woman behind her activity or station. Difficult to believe that Plato did not see it, that he deliberately quibbles and bullies poor Ion into all sorts of silly allegations, including the absurd one that he could be as great a general as anybody.

[1] Ojetti (1871–1946), novelist, playwright, and critic, was the regular literary columnist of the *Corriere*. The literary page ("*Tertza pagina*") played an important role in Italian newspapers, bringing literature into daily life.

93

20 JULY The *Timaeus* opens with a recapitulation of the idea in the *Republic* of a class of guardians. If one could hear Plato and one of the most enlightened seventeenth-century Jesuits discuss, it would be fun. The latter would have the logical advantage in not allowing the guardians to have wives and children. That would enable them to carry through a policy like theirs in Paraguay, which some day or other may again be tried somewhere, and with much greater chance of success, as there would be no wives or children intervening as a disturbing factor. If man lasts long enough on this planet, there is almost nothing conceivable that he will not try.

21 JULY Plato (*Philebus*, 23B Loeb 34–36) was well aware that civilizations perish because disasters following fast and faster leave only the unlettered to survive. These have no knowledge of what has happened, what has been attained before them. So here, too, I have been anticipated by Plato, for I came to the conclusion decades ago that what happened when a civilization declined was only that the cultured classes disappeared, leaving everything in the hands of the lowest group—the most numerous and, therefore, the survivors as a class.

22 JULY Cavour's diary from his twenty-fourth year.[2] So alive, so keen, so genuine, so free from all superstitions whatever—political or religious. Social? He sees nobody out of his own society, so one does not know. And withal a genuine gift as observer and writer—in short, a most promising young man and already a complete human being. Curiously, he makes more the impression of an Eng-

[2] Camillo Benso, conte di Cavour (1810–61): *Diario 1833–43* (Milan, 1941). Cavour, a leading statesman during the *Risorgimento* period, was largely responsible for achieving Italian unity under the House of Savoy.

lishman, or even American, than Italian, although he was probably more advanced than any Anglo-Saxon of a parallel class who was not a professional outcast like Byron or Shelley.

23 JULY Thackeray's *Pendennis*.[3] Good descriptive psychology, ironical, not satirical, and on the whole very good-humored. Delightful prose. Thackeray owes a good deal to Fielding, whom he modernizes, civilizes, and humanizes. Anticipates Dos Passos's "newsreel" technique, but uses it with discretion. Anticipates Laetitia's refusal of the "Egoist" in George Meredith. He makes Uncle Pendennis a jolly slattern, but fundamental aristocrats like Warrington or Pen's horsy college friend are done with affectionate sympathy. No sympathy with foreigners, however.

24 JULY The cosmic and human origins and mechanisms in Plato's *Timaeus* do not seem to rise above anthropology, except to the extent that a fine intellect is involved. Much of it as grotesque as Hindu thought, from which Plato may have got the notion of a karma which makes males who are naughty be reborn as females, or if still bad and worse, as lower and lower animals. Throughout, there is a certain unctuousness that easily leads over to sacramentalism and priestliness. Altogether a distasteful manifestation of the Hellenic mind.

25 JULY Voltaire's *Siècle de Louis XIV*.[4] Read for the first time since school days. Grievously disappointing.

[3] William Makepeace Thackeray: *Pendennis* (2 vols., London, 1910). The novel, which first appeared serially in 1848–50, is partly autobiographical; it draws on experiences he gained during his uncompleted studies of the law.
[4] Written in 1751, while Voltaire was living at the court of Frederick the Great.

No narration, just a series of notes about military and political matters. Improves when he gets to constitutional, social, and cultural questions. Takes great pain to show how serious he is, and no doubt he made many corrections to the then current notions; and he is really amazingly fair not only to the King but to Mme de Maintenon as well.[5] Seldom allows himself to be witty.

26 JULY Sir J. F. Stephen in his *Liberty, Equality, Fraternity* recounts that when a man was found dead in an English town before the reign of Edward III [1327–77], the community had to prove that the victim was not a Dane or, after the Norman Conquest, not a Frenchman, if it hoped to avoid the consequences. The book is suggestive and stimulating despite its paradoxes and its clubbing of liberal doctrines. He fights against their logic, forgetting that liberalism is a religion like every policy.[6]

27 JULY Long article by Jensen in *Paideuma* on Huizinga's *Homo Ludens*,[7] confined, however, chiefly to the interesting suggestion that all festivals and religious

[5] Mme de Maintenon (1635–1719) was the widow of the poet Paul Scarron; she rose from governess of the King's illegitimate children to a position of great prestige and influence in the court and, finally, became the King's second wife. She has long been quite unfairly held responsible for many of Louis's mistakes, particularly the revocation of the Edict of Nantes.

[6] Sir James Fitzjames Stephen (1829–94): *Liberty, Equality, Fraternity* (London, 1873). The title by no means indicates that the eminent jurist and man of letters approved of the French Revolutionary slogan; on the contrary, the work deplores the expansion of democracy and the diminishing of autocratic government.

[7] Johannes Jensen (1873–1950) was the Danish author, winner of the Nobel Prize for literature in 1944, who had a deep interest in folklore. Johan Huizinga's study, which has appeared in English as *Homo Ludens: The Role of Play in the Development of Culture* (Boston, 1955), was first published in Dutch in 1938 and in German the following year.

rites were a form of play. The author insists that play never loses consciousness of being play, whereas ritual and religious songs and festivals never—at least not in Jewish, Christian, and Islamic rituals—become consciously play, certainly not to the people. No doubt solemn religious processions like the Good Friday ones at Seville or Bari are as much enjoyed as play, but are surely not remotely taken for play.

28 JULY Ordered *L'Homme et le Péché* supposing it to be by Mauriac. He turns out to contribute but a few pages, these excellent on the silliness of the goody-goody novels offered to good boys and girls, and confessing that real novels have their roots in mud and worse, but that noble flowers may nevertheless appear.[8] ∼ Thérive, on "Le Péché de Bétise," [9] attacks the cults of anti-intellectualism, instinctivism, infantilism in all their phases, showing up their silliness, absurdity, and brutality, regarding them all as the last kick of Rousseauism.

29 JULY Atlantis as imagined by Plato in his *Critias* reminds me of Ledoux's scheme for an ideal city.[1] Only Ledoux was a practicing architect with a sense of material

[8] *L'Homme et le Péché* (Paris, 1938). Throughout his works, François Mauriac (1885–    ), the Catholic novelist, dramatist, and essayist, has been concerned with the exposure of mankind to the depths of evil in a Godless world and with the ultimate triumph of the divine spirit.

[9] In the same collection, the essay of André Thérive (1891–    ), novelist and critic, also reflects a long-time concern with the subject of sin: one of his early novels (1924) is *Le Plus Grand Péché*.

[1] Claude Nicolas Ledoux (1736–1806), who designed a number of palaces and public buildings in Paris, prepared elaborate plans for an ideal city ("Chaux"), to be built in the salt-mining district of Franche-Comté; the grand project was never realized. B. B. included a comment on Ledoux, and on *Critias*, in his Author's Foreword to this Diary.

97

possibilities whereas Plato, being first and last a poet, gives free rein to his imagination, which can be grotesque. He flies far, to Babylon perhaps, and returns with a plan of barbarous dimensions, proportions, splendor, and magnificence, preluding in its fantastic enormity the New Jerusalem of Revelation. It is not the Plato I most admire, nor is it the theosophist and remote and most unfortunate precursor, and to some measure creator, of Christian, particularly Catholic, theology, which still dominates the Church. Jesus could not have understood a word of it.

30 J U L Y Finished James Fitzjames Stephen's *Liberty, Equality, Fraternity*, a bumptious, vigorous, Philistine attack on those three terms of liberalism. Says many good and memorable things, and facts are to a great extent on his side, but he will not do justice to liberalism as an aspiration. It is not an impossible ideal, given human nature. Remains to be seen what is the least bad. He votes for stark Toryism. We would like to give liberalism as long a trial as Toryism has had hitherto.

31 J U L Y After nearly fifty years, I am rereading Pater's *Plato*.[2] Pater regrets that Socrates gave the Greeks a conscience, and then started their disintegration. I wonder could he have known Nietzsche or did he come to the same conclusion independently. Pater seems to know his author thoroughly and the commentators as well, yet he never becomes philological, remaining always humanistic, human, artistic even, drawing illustrations from poets and writers not only in England but also in France and in Germany. What a difference from any German book known to me on the same subject! Too much learning is a dangerous thing, as much as having too little!

[2] Walter Pater: *Plato and Platonism* (1893).

```
┌─────────────────────────────────────┐
│  ┌───────────────────────────────┐  │
│  │                               │  │
│  │      August 1942              │  │
│  │  ───────────────────────────  │  │
│  │                               │  │
│  │   S   M   T   W   T   F   S   │  │
│  │                               │  │
│  │   2   3   4   5   6   7  ⅛    │  │
│  │                               │  │
│  │   9  10  11  12  13  14  15   │  │
│  │                               │  │
│  │  16  17  18  19  20  21  22   │  │
│  │                               │  │
│  │  ²³/₃₀ ²⁴/₃₁ 25 26 27 28 29   │  │
│  │                               │  │
│  └───────────────────────────────┘  │
└─────────────────────────────────────┘
```

1 AUGUST Seldom read anything so convincing, so touching, so inspiring as the seventh of Plato's *Epistles*. Speaks of what was best in his thoughts as beyond words, and to be understood, or only preserved, in flashes of vision. His relations with the youthful despot Dionysius are described with the art of a novelist. One sees the young wretch who, if a Roman, would be a Caligula, but who, being a Hellene, retains a certain respect for cultured opinion. ~ A. E. Taylor's essay on Plato could scarcely be better, given the space.[3] A singularly clear, comprehensive account, proving again that it takes a real scholar and thinker to write briefly on a great subject, for he alone can afford to soar over the whole landscape, picking out the salient points, giving each its value, ignoring the rest. Taylor's estimates

[3] *Platonism and Its Influence* (London, 1925). Taylor (1869–1945) was professor of moral philosophy at Edinburgh. His Greek studies and history of philosophy are now standard sources.

99

are admirable. How I regret that I possess none of his detailed studies of Plato!

2 AUGUST Finishing Thackeray's *Pendennis*, the most genial, the least sneering, least sardonic of his novels. Never more than descriptive, as of a landscape with its storm and sunshine but no geological, no meteorological inquiries. Delightful description of Derby Day, its crowds of every shape and color and humor. I wonder whether it was done before or after Frith's so popular picture.[4] Independent of each other they scarcely can be, though Thackeray's creation is superior as a work of art.

3 AUGUST Plato in introducing Charmides[5] speaks of his beautiful face; yet if one could strip him and see him nude, he says, one would forget his face. This accords with what I have thought for a long time, and must have said in print somewhere, that when a statue is beautiful you do not miss the head. I went so far as to suggest that if you wanted to judge of a figure, you should begin by mentally decapitating it. As I read Plato, I am again and again struck by the way he anticipated us in feeling, thinking, and appreciating.

4 AUGUST Before beginning Plato's *Alcibiades* read the introduction in Loeb Classics, where scarcely a word is said about its authenticity. On the contrary, Geffcken in his *Griechische Literatur-Geschichte* speaks with contempt of those who still regard it as genuine.[6] It reads like the

---

[4] "Derby Day," by William Powell Frith (1819–1909), hangs in the National Gallery, London. It was painted about 1859; *Pendennis* was completed in 1850.

[5] In his Dialogue of the same name.

[6] Johannes Geffcken (born 1861) was professor of classical philology at Rostock University. His history of Greek literature was published at Heidelberg (Vol. I, 1926; Vol. II, 1934). Contempo-

attack I would make on anyone who still ascribed certain manifest imitations of Giorgione or Botticelli to those masters themselves. As market values are not engaged, controversies over authenticity in matters literary do not rouse public curiosity as they do where works of art are concerned.

5 AUGUST Looking back on *Pendennis*, it seems the sanest, least sardonic, least preachy of his novels. Old Pendennis stands out as a complete pagan Englishman of the marginal class. Lady Rockminister is the perfect specimen of the great English lady with her *franc parler*. Strong and Morgan are each perfect in his way; and Blanche, Focker, Fanny, and Huckster are not overdone. Of course, young Pendennis is the least consistent, the least alive. The central figure in a novel seldom is the most congruous and convincing.

6 AUGUST Finished *Alcibiades I*, and cannot see why either as thought or language it is not by Plato. Probably I am not competent enough in either field, and fail to perceive what specialists penetrate with security. It is parallel with my detaching certain pictures from great masters even though the plea is that they are but tentative and immature works. I recognize, on the contrary, that they are imitations. ⁓ Finished also Pater's *Plato*. "Lacedemon" too much influenced by K. O. Müller's romantic picture,[7] which can have but faint resemblance to what the actuality must have been.

---

rary scholars seem universally agreed that, of the works attributed to Plato, the following are not genuine: *Alcibiades I* and *II*, *Cleitrophro*, *Erastae*, *Hipparchus*, *Minos*, and *Theages*.

[7] Karl Otfried Müller (1791–1840): *Literature of Ancient Greece* (London, 1850), translation from unpublished German text (1840). Müller was the Göttingen classical scholar and archeologist.

7 AUGUST Platonic *Alcibiades II*. Almost Christian, and even more Jewish, in its attitude toward sacrifice and prayer, and pure hearts rather than hecatombs, and regrets for nothing in particular but for what the gods know to be good for us. ⁓ Weidlé in *L'Homme et le Péché*, on the growing pride and arrogance of the artist and his separating himself off more and more from the public, develops admirably what has been in my mind on the subject for several decades. Pity it appears in a volume so unlikely to reach the public, or the artists.[8]

8 AUGUST More of Friedrich Schlegel's aphorisms and fragments. Am again amazed at his precocity in a field where that is so rare, criticism. At twenty-two and twenty-three he affirms opinions to which I came of myself in my maturest years. He indeed was a precursor in critical sensitiveness as well as in thinking—a real *Vorschmecker*. He alone had the courage to proclaim the value of indolence, of lying fallow, letting *Einfälle* occur to enlarge and enrich one with ideas, instead of following out with industry one's own very few ideas.

9 AUGUST *Erlebnisse eines Schweizerarztes bei den türkischen Nazionalisten*, published in 1921,[9] recounts what went on at Urfa during the revival of Turko-Macedonian fanaticism. The treachery of the Turks, pretending they had nothing to do with the measures of the French that they had obviously arranged. Sad lights on brainlessness of

[8] Wladimir Weidlé (1895–    ), a Russian student of Byzantine art, has lectured in Paris since 1932. His contribution to the volume was entitled "L'Orgueil Déchéance de l'Homme Créateur."

[9] The Swiss doctor was Andreas Vischer (1877–1930). He served in Urfa, in East Turkey, with the German Oriental Mission Hospital from 1905 to 1914 and, in 1919–20, with the remaining Armenians and the French garrison.

French government, which had no idea of what forces it would need to assert itself in the Near East. Its cowardly arrangements with the Turks, to the extent even of furnishing them with arms against the Greeks. Some pages read as if taken out of Werfel's *Musa Dagh.*[1]

10 AUGUST After many years, reread in Pater's *Greek Studies* essays on Demeter and on Hippolytus.[2] They still hold their own. I appreciate the extraordinary and minute learning behind the elaborate style, with its successful effects of aloofness and its bas-relief-like form. Nevertheless, a singularly convincing atmosphere prevails that removes them from anything artificial, let alone pedantic. Curious how little the style changes in the years between these essays; those on the Renaissance coming in between are very similar in intonation and phrasing.

11 AUGUST "How has it ever come about, Socrates, that this report is spread of Minos, as an uneducated and harsh-tempered person?" Socrates answers: "Because of something that will make both of you, if you are wise, and everybody else who cares to have a good reputation, beware of ever quarreling with any man of a poetic turn. For poets have great influence over opinion, according as they create it in the minds of men either by commending or vilifying." (Platonic *Minos*, 320 E.) So the author of that dialogue was as well aware as we are of the propaganda value of

[1] *The Forty Days of Musa Dagh* (1934) was the best-selling novel based on the heroic resistance of the Armenians against the Turks in World War I. Franz Werfel (1890–1945) was an Austrian novelist, dramatist, and poet who fled to France and then to America after the Nazi occupations.
[2] "The Myth of Demeter and Persephone" (1876) and "Hippolytus Unveiled" (1889) are included in the posthumous *Greek Studies* (London, 1895).

literature as, *a fortiori,* he would have been were he acquainted with the daily papers and the radio. Indeed, it is a problem that has preoccupied me since my youth—how to tame publicity of every sort, and make it an instrument for good only.

12 AUGUST Stokoe's *German Influence in the English Romantic Period.*[3] A dull book, little more than statistical. Tends to diminish the amount of that influence except in the case of Coleridge as philosopher. I had hoped to discover that Shelley was acquainted with the second *Faust,* where the lyrical parts have rhythms undulating and aerial that have always reminded me of his. Apparently not—and yet how account for such a startling similarity, although iso-psychicism can do strange things, and why not in the case of prosody as well!

13 AUGUST Pater on Greek sculpture before Phidias,[4] not only as accurate an account as could be given in his day—accurate without being minute—not only beautifully written, but inspired by the will to communicate to the reader, not so much what he knew, but what he felt about early Greek sculpture. The trouble with professional archeologists and historians of Greek art is that they almost never touch on it as a vital experience, toward which all their study and research should contribute.

14 AUGUST *The Pre-Raphaelite Tragedy* by William Gaunt[5] begins too smartly and superironically after the

---

[3] Frank W. Stokoe (1882–    ): *German Influence in the English Romantic Period, 1788–1818* (Cambridge, 1926).
[4] "The Beginnings of Greek Sculpture" (1880) and "The Marbles of Aegina" (1880) are also in *Greek Studies.*
[5] Gaunt (1900–    ) has written extensively on art and social history and has been art critic for the *Evening Standard* and *Punch.* This work (1942) is the first of his series on nineteenth-century art and artists.

Lytton Strachey model. But when the writer gets hold of the subject, he forgets all that and gives a vivid account of the movement and above all of the personalities involved, doing fair justice all around. It falls down where so many English books do, in scarcely touching on the ideas which lie behind every movement. The author does not seem fully or indeed adequately aware of how deep as well as pervasive [Dante Gabriel] Rossetti's influence was throughout.

15 AUGUST From my youth, I cherished a strong desire to visit Cyrene. I have often asked myself how I came by it. This morning in *Marius the Epicurean* [6] I found the passage which almost certainly inoculated me with the longing to see and explore Cyrene. I wonder whether Dick Norton owed his inspiration to the same source. He, being a man of action, led an expedition thither, the which excited the fear of Italian nationalists that the U.S.A. meant to acquire Cyrene.[7] They could not conceive of an expedition without a political aim.

16 AUGUST Rereading Pater's *Marius*, I am surprised to discover to what extent it is my own spiritual biography. Its direct influence on me was no doubt great. Still, no outside influence could have affected me so deeply, pervasively, and permanently if the current of my spirit had not been

---

[6] London, 1882; generally considered Walter Pater's masterpiece.
[7] Richard Norton's expedition (1910–11) is described in the *Bulletin of the Archaeological Society of America* (ii, 1911). Cyrene was a Greek colony, founded about 630 B.C., on the northern coast of Africa directly across the Mediterranean from the southernmost tip of Greece. It became a large and beautiful city and was an important cultural and commercial center. The Italian concern in 1911 arose from the monarchy's then current dispute with Turkey over Libya, of which the Cyrene area is a part. Richard Norton (1872–1918) was the son of Charles Eliot Norton.

in the same direction. Surely I read and reread much else at that time, but never when rereading have I felt myself so identified with the thoughts, aspirations, doubts, and consents that I rediscover in *Marius.*

17 AUGUST Began Abbate Ricciotti's *Vita di Gesù.*[8] Historical part, chiefly about Herod and his descendants, irreproachable and excellent in tone. So, too, his account of Pharisaical Judaism as then practiced—fair and quite adequate for his purpose. He writes easily, that is to say, it is pleasant, cursive reading. I look forward with curiosity to see what he will make of modern criticism of the sources. I see already that he means to tackle Renan and Loisy.[9] It will be fun to measure the length of the string by which he is tied to orthodoxy.

18 AUGUST Finished Voltaire's *Siècle de Louis XIV.* Third volume most interesting because author takes malicious delight in recounting the squabbles of the various sects within the Church. He is singularly cool in his account of literature, and says practically nothing about the arts. Fair on administration. But throughout no current of narrative, no glow. Rather a series of notes and observations following each other in loose sequence under certain rubrics. So I cannot understand why in my youth it still counted as a masterpiece of historical writing.

19 AUGUST Reading C. T. Newton's account of his life and researches in the Levant in the 1850's.[1] A keen ar-

[8] Milan, 1941. Abbot Giuseppe Ricciotti (1890–   ) is a theologian, philologist, archeologist, and Semitic scholar.
[9] Ernest Renan (1823–92) and Alfred Firmin Loisy (1857–1940) are representatives of those biblical critics who have turned from the religious to the historical approach. Loisy became the principal leader of the Catholic Modernism movement.
[1] Sir Charles Thomas Newton (1816–94): *Travels and Discoveries in the Levant* (2 vols., London, 1865). The noted Greek scholar

cheologist, he is an observer of life and gives entertaining accounts of Greek habits and morals, as well as of Turkish incompetence, corruption, and misrule—yet on the whole less repulsive than Greek trickery. A story of *vendetta* as gruesome as any in the volumes of short stories Bacchelli has just sent me. This Newton was the teacher of our oldest surviving enemy friend, Eugénie Strong.[2]

20 AUGUST Three small volumes of short stories by Bacchelli.[3] Unlike most Italian writers, he can narrate and construct. Has an amazing vocabulary, not rare or precious, but vital and swift. Immense anthropological and prehistorical knowledge. A fine vein of allegory. "The Case of the Mary Bounfield" is the story of a ship in which none are left but three sailors. Then the rats take command and the sailors become the slaves. *"Torre Lunare"* tells of savages who build a tower to reach the Moon; when their material is used up, someone advises them to take the stones out of the base to put on the top.

21 AUGUST Charles Ricketts's *Unrecorded Histories,*[4] pastiches in the manner of Anatole France, but which

---

was keeper of classical antiquities at the British Museum (1862–85) and was responsible for many important acquisitions.

[2] Eugénie Sellers Strong lectured at the British Museum early in her career and was later, for many years, assistant director of the British School of Archeology in Rome. She died in the year following this Diary.

[3] *L'Elmo di Tancredi ed altre Novelle giocose; La Fine di Atlantide ed altre Favole lunatiche; Il Brigante di Tacca di Lupo ed altri Racconti disperati.* All three volumes were published in Milan in 1942. Riccardo Bacchelli (1891–    ) has been a successful historical novelist as well as a short-story writer and poet. He is a powerful stylist and a conscious classicist.

[4] London, 1933. Ricketts (1866–1931), in addition to his career as a painter, was a noted illustrator of books, designer for the stage, and printer (founder of the Vale Press, one of the several great fine-printing establishments in London around the turn of the century).

I cannot resist perusing and enjoying, as I do almost anything in the way of imaginary conversation, particularly
when it deals with antiquity. Here, as in his painting, Ricketts knows exactly what ought to be done, but cannot
vitalize anything. Yet what a gifted and cultured man he
was—far beyond any other English contemporary of mine
in the field of art.

22 AUGUST Essay by Mario Praz on Chaucer and
Italy,[5] philological and historical of the best. He makes it
plausible that Chaucer was but slightly acquainted with
Boccaccio, and that on the other hand he knew his Dante
most intimately, using him on every suitable occasion. Praz
reveals to me the vast literature that has sprung up over
the question of Chaucer's sources—as if they alone made
Chaucer worth studying. Perhaps poets and all other artists
cannot be studied otherwise, and therefore should not be
studied at all, except, of course, to furnish bread and butter
and vanity to the students. Do they ever help us to enjoy,
I wonder.

23 AUGUST Mary read aloud chapter on Jerusalem
in Kinglake's *Eothen*.[6] It sounded a little cheap and juve-
nile, unfortunately. It was one of our pet memories. This
time it seemed so inferior to what I remember of Gérard

[5] "*Chaucer e i grandi Trecentisti Italiani*" (1927) in *Macchiavelli
in Inghilterra ed altri Saggi* (Rome, 1942). Praz, born in Italy in
1896, went to England in 1923 and taught at the universities of
Liverpool and Manchester. He is now professor of English language and literature at the University of Rome. He has written
widely on the literature and literary figures of both England and
the Continent; his controversial *Romantic Agony*, which first appeared in English in 1933, was reissued in 1956.
[6] Alexander William Kinglake (1809–91): *Eothen* (1844). An English traveler and historian, Kinglake in this book set down a classic
account of his journey in 1835 to the Far East.

de Nerval.[7] Interesting his insistence that all members of the Orthodox Church feel obliged to attend the Pascal Feast in Jerusalem at least once in their lives—a duty taken over from Jewry, which no doubt imposed it on all Jews no matter where living. Few days pass without my reading of some Christian dogma, rite, or usage taken over, or rather flowing down, from its source—the ancient synagogue.

24 AUGUST Pater's picture of nascent or rather emerging Christianity not only overidealized, but unhistorical, describes a condition of things that were thus shaped centuries later. So this successor of Telemachus and Anacharsis, this *Marius the Epicurean,* is too easily won over to the ritual, to the décor of Pater's wishful reconstruction of early Christianity. True, he exhibits it in a princely domain and in the most refined surroundings, and at a service as captivating to Marius' spirit as possible. He should have gone further afield and inquired how it worked elsewhere.

25 AUGUST Praz's most learned and surprising essay on Machiavelli in Elizabethan England,[8] makes out that much of what is called Machiavellianism was inculcated by Seneca long before Machiavelli was known in England. But surely Plato too, in the *Republic* and elsewhere, gives a good statement of what the unprejudiced politician out for power is ready to do. To me it was new that Machiavelli was held responsible for Catherine de' Medici and her gang of Florentines, as well as for Loyola and Jesuitism. Indeed,

---

[7] Nerval (1808–55), was a poet and writer of fantasies. A bohemian and *noctambule,* he was a member of the younger group of French romantics; his travel sketches included the account of a trip to Jerusalem (in *Voyage en Orient*).

[8] Written in 1929–30, the essay appears in Mario Praz's *Macchiavelli in Inghilterra.*

Machiavelli and Loyola, Machiavellianism and Jesuitism, got telescoped as one horrid, hellish movement for the suppression of decency, freedom, and any kind of humanity.

26 AUGUST Pater's "Child in the House" and "Emerald Uthwart" [9] give a picture of the ideal English youth, healthy, simple-minded, unquestioning, but high-spirited, though sensitive, enjoying beauty unwittingly and the ritual of life unconsciously. He is ever being prepared to take part in politics, or soldiering, or higher business—to conduct his career as a gentleman first and foremost. He made the England we have loved, which was still intact in my first contacts with it fifty-five years ago.

27 AUGUST Jowett's introduction and analysis of Plato's *Republic* [1]—230 small-print octavo pages. Am amazed at the lucidity of the analyses, and the good sense, liberality, and even courage of the comments. Not shaken by the suggestions regarding communal property. On the contrary, he discusses them sympathetically. So in matters of education and religion, he is on the side of progress in every direction. Again and again a delicate irony dictates his comments, and once in a great while he permits himself to be outright witty. To me profitable as well as entertaining.

28 AUGUST Read with keenest interest the second volume of C. T. Newton's *Travels in the Levant*, his ac-

[9] Dated 1879 and 1892, respectively, the essays appear in Walter Pater's *Miscellaneous Studies*, published posthumously (London, 1895).
[1] Benjamin Jowett (1817–93): "Introduction and Analysis" to *The Republic*, in Volume III of *The Dialogues of Plato* (5 vols., Oxford, 1892). Jowett, a theologian and one of the greatest Greek scholars, was Master of Balliol College at Oxford.

count of the rediscovery and excavation of the mausoleum at Cnidos and Branchidae. What exciting fun it must have been. The visitor who now sees the results in the British Museum is little aware of what they cost and what they gave in return. Better perhaps than archeological information and aesthetic evaluation in catalogues would it be if they quoted some of the most vivid passages in the reports or writings of the discoverers of the antiquities in question.

29 AUGUST Van Wyck Brooks on Emerson, based on latter's diaries, gives an excellent picture of Emerson and his paladins.[2] To Mary and me, it is full of touching reminiscences of what we as youngsters heard from our elders. Reading about the Concord circle now, I realize how much I, despite my foreign birth and childhood, despite all superposed impressions of fifty-five years of living away from America, owe to those New England precursors—most of my brain values, many of my prejudices, and any number of my hopes and fears.

30 AUGUST Began Dickens's *Our Mutual Friend*.[3] Opening chapter sinister and evocative to the last degree *but* followed by a caricature of High Life performed by wooden marionettes badly carved and worse colored. I have in the course of the last sixty years tried Dickens again and again, felt overwhelmed by the opening, only to be let down immediately into the mud or worse. I do not question Dickens's native gift, but his way of using it is to me revolting, the more so as the English are so devoted to him.[4]

[2] Van Wyck Brooks (1886–    ): *Emerson and Others* (New York, 1927).
[3] Dickens's last finished novel (1865).
[4] Two years later, however, B. B. was to note: "One must try again and again. Only now in advanced age have I got to enjoy Dickens, although I have not yet become an ardent admirer."

31 AUGUST Finished Reininger's *Kant*,[5] a succinct, but as seems to me comprehensive, account of Kant's career as a thinker and writer and of his influence on the thought of Europe ever since. From my college days on, it has always seemed to me that Kant's view of the universe, of the knowable and unknowable, were mine from my earliest years, as if born to it or acquiring it in childhood *par osmose*, so that I have never been able to shake it off, even when trying hard. ⌒ I read Kant and his ilk with the hope of getting light on a problem that worries me. It is the word "nature" and what is behind it. Thus far, neither Kant nor any other has helped me. We contrast "art" and "nature," and speak of art as having this or that relation to nature. What art is, we know more or less, for we have made it, as we have made more exact sciences, even all mathematics, out of inexpugnable notions of our mind. But Nature? Who is she and where to find her?

[5] *Kant, seine Anhänger und seine Gegner* (Munich, 1923) is by Robert Reininger, who was professor of philosophy at the University of Vienna in the period before World War II.

```
┌─────────────────────────────────────┐
│  ┌───────────────────────────────┐  │
│  │                               │  │
│  │     September 1942            │  │
│  │  ───────────────────────────  │  │
│  │                               │  │
│  │   S  M  T  W  T  F  S         │  │
│  │                               │  │
│  │            1  2  3  4  5      │  │
│  │                               │  │
│  │   6  7  8  9  10 11 12        │  │
│  │                               │  │
│  │   13 14 15 16 17 18 19        │  │
│  │                               │  │
│  │  20/ 21/ 22/ 23/ 24 25 26     │  │
│  │   27  28  29  30              │  │
│  │                               │  │
│  └───────────────────────────────┘  │
└─────────────────────────────────────┘
```

1 SEPTEMBER Huxley's *Hume,* rather Philistinish in its cocksure materialism, but informing, stimulating, and in its way constructive.[6] I am not surprised to discover how natural the British approach to the problems of knowledge is to me. I suppose I owe it partly to my own brains and partly to the atmosphere in which my formative years were passed. On the other hand, the post-Kantian German metaphysics is utterly beyond me, and while I cannot resist dipping into it, I get no refreshment from it.

2 SEPTEMBER Article in last *Critica d'Arte*[7] by Massimo Pallottino on Mycenaean foundation of Greek

[6] Thomas Henry Huxley (1825–95) was more than a great biologist and energetic supporter of Darwin; his wide range of writings included works on "man's place in nature," on the relationships between science and culture, on morals and ethics, and on philosophy in general. His study of David Hume was written in 1879, about a century after the death of the Scottish philosopher.

[7] *La Critica d'Arte,* a quarterly "review of the figurative art of the ancient world," was published in Florence from 1935 to 1942.

113

archaic art. To me quite patent, as I perceived after studying remains in Crete as well as on the Continent. Internal
fatigue and reaction against the riot of lassoing cuttlefishes
and cakewalking attitudes led to geometrization, without
the need of assuming that a far more primitive stage of art,
a new style, could arise only when one population replaced
another. All the art phenomena of preclassical Greece can
be explained without Doric invasion.

3 SEPTEMBER Disappointed with Plato's treatment
of art in Book X of *The Republic.* In poetry he finds
imitation of feeling, which certainly is better than mere
"photographic" reproduction, which is all he grants to visual art. All arising from the dogma that art is but imitation
or reproduction of a celestial model. Plato surely knew
better, but could not do justice to his own better knowledge
owing to obstinacy in maintaining the doctrine of ideas.

4 SEPTEMBER Peter Meyer, Zürich architect, reviews Wilhelm Pinder's *Kunst der deutschen Kaiserzeit.*[8]
He points out how the author falsifies and misinterprets in
order to give Germany primacy in the arts. Thus, as Pinder
cannot claim Gothic as German, he belittles and discards
it as a deplorable deviation from the noble and serene severity of Romanesque, to which he sets claim as not being
exactly of German origin but as having reached its highest
in Germany, particularly through achieving greater plas-
ticity than anywhere else—an opinion which Meyer proves
untenable.

[8] *Die Kunst der deutschen Kaiserzeit bis zum Ende der staufischen
Klassik* (1935), in *Das Werk, Jahrgang XXIII* (Zürich, 1936). Pinder (1878–1947) was professor of art history at several leading
German universities. Meyer (1894–    ), an art critic as well as an
architect, has been lecturer on European art and on the history of
style at Zürich University and Polytechnic.

5 SEPTEMBER *Il Mercante di Quadri* by Raffaello Franchi,[9] a collection presumably of short stories but really of elegies in prose—subtle, delicate, at times profound, mostly enigmatic, even cryptic, except the last. Although equally enigmatic, it is the only real short story, something between Nathaniel Hawthorne and Villiers de l'Isle-Adam.[1] Altogether an interesting if rather overprecious achievement, leaving behind almost everything of the same genre that I can recall reading recently in French. I wonder how many will peruse it and appreciate it even to the degree that I have.

6 SEPTEMBER Began Albert Béguin's *L'Âme romantique et le Rêve,*[2] and do not see yet what he is driving at. But it has already provided information about Philipp Moritz quite new to me.[3] Have known him only in his travels in England where, however, I recollect no note of intense self-analysis leading to mysticism. He seems to have tried to substantiate the Wordsworthian "Our birth is but a sleep and a forgetting," and the famous ode must express what he was aiming at better than he himself could say. But Béguin seems in characteristic "Latin" way unaware of Wordsworth's existence or indeed of any of the English romantics, Platonists, or mystics.

[9] Florence, 1942. Franchi (1899–1949) was an art and literary critic as well as a writer of fiction; he contributed to several of the Italian literary reviews.
[1] *Contes cruels* (1883) is the best-known collection of fantastic and macabre short stories of Comte de Villiers de l'Isle-Adam (1838–89).
[2] Paris, 1939. Béguin (1901–    ), a linguist and critic, has especially explored the use of mysticism in poetry.
[3] (Karl) Philipp Moritz (1756–93), a friend of Goethe, was a prolific writer and a man of complex temperament. His crowded career embraced the stage and the church, linguistics and literary criticism.

7 SEPTEMBER Read in *Deutsche Biographie*
L. Geiger's article on Philipp Moritz. One would scarcely
know one was reading about the same Moritz as described
by Béguin. The last ignores his subject's manifold activities
in many active as well as literary fields, leaving some forty
or more volumes behind him when he died while still in
his thirties, to speak only of his abnormal psychology, his
spooky side. Béguin mentions Lichtenberg without falsify-
ing the picture quite as much.[4] I am beginning to see that
Béguin, in speaking of *le rêve*, does not mean dreams in a
merely poetical sense, but literally the dreams that come to
one during the hours of sleep.

8 SEPTEMBER Finished Jowett's analysis and introduction to *Timaeus*.[5] Sound sense, sympathy, but not idol-
atry. To me, Plato's cosmology seems like the last word in
primitive thought, as Minoan was the last achievement of
primitive—that is, spontaneous, preintellectual, precanoni-
cal—art. As for so much of his dialectic and his "ideas," I
am sure I passed through phases of cerebration and mus-
ing when similar methods and abstractions occurred to me
in the years between early childhood and youth. Of course,
I should be considered a monster of conceit and impudence
if I declared in public that most of Plato's philosophy is
adolescent, and that it is his style and his wisdom and his
dialectics that make us—even those of us who are not
superstitious about metaphysics—take it with such solemn
seriousness.

[4] Georg Christoph Lichtenberg (1742–99) was another of Béguin's
subjects with an improbable career. A professor of physics whose
special field was electricity, he made several visits to England and
became a satirist under Swift's influence; he also wrote on Hogarth's etchings.
[5] In Volume III of his edition of *The Dialogues of Plato*.

116

9 SEPTEMBER *Madame de Staël et François de Pange* by Comtesse Jean de Pange.[6] François seems to have been one of the clearest political thinkers of the Revolution. Mme de Staël seems to have loved him with an all-absorbing passion, not affected even by his marriage, and despite the fact that Benjamin Constant was already with her. What eloquence, what convincing sincerity in her letters to De Pange! I know of no other woman about whom, as of Napoleon or Goethe, one never tires of reading in the hope of learning more. Always rewarded by contact with a vitalizing personality.

10 SEPTEMBER Marie-Laure de Noailles in *La Tour de Babel* (pages 38–39): "*L'arbre de la science, hérissé d'épines pensives, tordu tel le baobab, fouillait le mystère nocturne de ses branches acérées, gonflées de l'encre amère des philosophes; l'écorce craquait sous la poussée permanente des casualités, tandis que les termites diligents attaquaient la volonté incorruptible des belles racines, qui s'enfonçaient dans 'la matière.'*" It is the "Other" who has attached to it the "forbidden" fruit. Jehovah warns them that if they eat thereof they will die. Eve: "*Est-ce terrible de mourir?*" Jehovah does not confess that he does not know what it is to die, that it was the business of the "Other." "*Il certifie l'horreur de la chose, traitant ainsi la femme comme la petite fille qu'elle n'avait jamais eté encore.*" [7] The like of this makes it worth while to go through a book in which there is far too much "*cocasserie.*"

---

[6] The book was published in Paris in 1925. Like the Comtesse's book on Mme de Staël and A. W. Schlegel (see March 11), it is based on previously unpublished letters and documents.
[7] "The Tree of Knowledge was covered with the thorns of abstract thought and twisted like a baobab; its sharp branches, swollen with philosophy's bitter ink, pierced the nocturnal mystery; the bark was cracking under the continuous pressure of fortuitous events.

11 SEPTEMBER Emil Sulger-Gebing's excellent account of the brothers Schlegel and their *"Verhältnisse zur bildenden Kunst."* [8] In earlier years, Friedrich was more my precursor than anyone else I have ever read or heard of. Later he took to a merely Roman Catholic interpretation and was the effective forerunner of Rio [9] and others of that kind. Friedrich no doubt despised the *Nazarener*. August Wilhelm, though far less gifted, was more true to his earlier ideals on the whole, even if he too got more and more absorbed in *"Deutsche Kunst."* In 1843 he writes to Prince Albert [Victoria's consort] requesting assistance for completion of the Cologne Cathedral. The interesting answer is that the Prince gladly would, but dares not because the state of [British] public opinion about Church matters is so ticklish that his act would be misinterpreted.

12 SEPTEMBER Rereading Pater, and reading Jowett's comments on the various dialogues of Plato makes me realize, although always aware of it, how much I am an earth-and-time bubble of my generation. Both seem so intimately to say what I go on feeling so many years after their works were published, while the things of today are at best outside and at worst either unintelligible or repellent. Yet I am more open than most to newness, to otherness, to wrenching my neck so as to free my head to look around.

---

Meanwhile, eager termites were trying to undermine the perfect will of the beautiful roots sunk deeply into the earth of the material world." The final lines may be translated: "He assures her of the horror of death, and in this way he treats the woman as the little girl she never was." The book, published at Clermont-Ferrand in 1942, is by the wife of Charles, vicomte de Noailles. The Noailles villa at Hyères has been a center for writers and musicians.

[8] *Die Brüder August Wilhelm und Friedrich Schlegel in ihrem Verhältnisse zur bildenden Kunst* (Munich, 1897).

[9] Alexis François Rio (1797–1874) was the author of *Christian Art* (1841–55) and *Ancient Ideal and Christian Ideal* (1873).

13 SEPTEMBER Dickens tends to reduce everything to genre—tragedy, comedy, farce, everything except those petty law clerks known in his day as actuaries. These he succeeds in making ominous. Character is purely descriptive from the outside, never analytical, never soul-searching, seldom in immediate relation to the imponderable, the demoniacal, the superhuman of which he can give such wonderful evocations, as bravado pieces. His comedy rapidly turns to farce, and personages to types—so caricatured that the meanest intelligence cannot fail to spot them. He helps himself out with repetition that stamps his figures on our memories.

14 SEPTEMBER The scene in *Mutual Friend* between Eugene Wrayburn, on the one hand, and Charley Hexham, on the other, is a masterpiece. The blustering although sincere enough earnestness of the latter is wonderfully contrasted with the elegant insolence of the former. Where did he see him, a type so much genre of the 1890's and later. Indeed, Eugene talks and acts exactly the way Oscar Wilde did the last time I saw him and tried to persuade him to drop "Bosie." [1] Very fine as well is the old Jew who, as a saint and gentleman, slaves for Fledgeby out of gratitude for the kindness shown him by Fledgeby's father.

15 SEPTEMBER Finished Marie-Laure's *Tour de Babel*—as cryptic, allusive, illusive, absurd, indecent, disgusting, eloquent, penetrating, profound as any apocalyptic

---

[1] "Bosie" was Lord Alfred Douglas (1870–1945), the poet whose relationship with Wilde (twenty-five years his senior) led to the notorious trial in which Wilde sued Douglas's father, the Marquess of Queensberry, for libel. Although Wilde soon dropped the suit, evidence introduced in it resulted in his conviction for immoral conduct (1895) and his term in Reading Gaol.

stuff from Ezekiel through the Second Ezra, Enoch, Daniel, Revelation, and the Sibylline and Gnostic prophecies. Added is the irony of Anatole France and the *"cocasserie"* of Jean Cocteau. What it is all about I cannot make out, although through chinks I see light here and there. There are sonorous and almost magnificent bits of writing. ~ Mary read out from Ticknor's diaries during his first "grand tour." Amazing whom he met, and how he was received! [2]

16 SEPTEMBER Pater's *Gaston Latour*,[3] chiefly interesting for portraits of Ronsard and Montaigne—the latter particularly successful—and one not so happy of Giordano Bruno. Pater presents them for us to interpret, not intervening with attempts to penetrate character with ready-made formulas after Taine's fashion, followed since by most critics everywhere. Pater lets us live with Ronsard and Montaigne, and we part with them as after an actual experience, and not a mere description.

17 SEPTEMBER Was rather bored with Béguin's *L'Âme romantique et le Rêve* so long as he wrote of the people who, according to him, made a business of the dream-world on its own account. Now that he has come to the famous writers, I like him better. The chapters on Novalis and Tieck which I have already perused interested me, although Béguin there too emphasizes the lunar, the

[2] George Ticknor (1791–1871): *Life, Letters, and Journals* (2 vols., Boston, 1876). The tour was an extensive one: it began in 1815 when Ticknor and Edward Everett left Boston to study at Göttingen. Ticknor continued on to study languages and instruction methods elsewhere in Germany and in Italy, Spain, Portugal, and England. In 1819, he returned to Harvard and introduced important innovations in language teaching.

[3] Walter Pater's unfinished historical romance, *Gaston de Latour*, was published posthumously in London in 1896.

will-o'-the-wisp, the fairy, the nostalgic, the unsatisfiable, the yearning for the unearthly in the writings of both. Still I am glad to renew my acquaintance with them through this pale-blue glass window.[4]

18 SEPTEMBER Remarkable paper by Peter Meyer, *"Die Bedeutung der 'Rasse' in der Architektur-Geschichte."* Never before encountered such perfect expression in a few words of all I think of such matter with regard to history in general and art-history in particular. He characterizes the adaptation to taste of invaders as follows: *"Es bedeutet stets ein Zurückübersetzen des Artikulierten ins Unartikulierte, des individualisierten ins Kontinuum. Das Relief wird zum Teppichmuster, die Figur zum Ornament, das plastische Architekturglied zum flachen Relief."* [5] Barbarians did renew energy, but "transfusion of blood to a patient . . . has no effect on assimilating the patient to the blood-giver."

19 SEPTEMBER Van Wyck Brooks's *Flowering of New England* [6] and Ticknor's and Prescott's letters.[7]

[4] Novalis was the pseudonym of Georg Friedrich Philipp von Hardenberg, who studied philosophy under Schiller, Friedrich Schlegel, and Fichte; he was especially influenced by Fichte. The poet's career was a short one; he was born in 1772 and died of tuberculosis at only twenty-nine, leaving unfinished his single novel, *Heinrich von Ofterdingen,* considered the representative novel of early German romanticism. On Tieck, see Note 6 under January 10.
[5] "It always leads to reducing the articulate to the inarticulate, the individualized to the generalized style. The relief becomes a tapestry pattern, the figure an ornament, the structural feature in architecture a flat relief." The paper appears in *Schweizerische Bauzeitung* (Zürich, 1933).
[6] New York, 1936, 1957. The period covered is 1815–65.
[7] In Volume II of Ticknor's *Life, Letters, and Journals.* William H. Prescott (1796–1859) was the great Boston historian of the Mexican and Peruvian conquests. Half-blind, he relied on his intimate friend Ticknor for manuscript and proof revisions of his works.

They have for Mary and me an intimacy and warmth of interest explicable only through our spiritual origins. They are us before we were born—but *us*. The experience helps us to understand our Italian and French friends, with their absorbing preoccupation with thinkers and writers almost purely local, offering nothing to foreigners that these do not already have of their own—as good in quality and as important in kind. But the foreigner should not try to share their enthusiasm.

20 SEPTEMBER Had no idea Eichendorff was so interesting a poet as Béguin makes him out. Turned to Stefan George's selection and discovered several poems of great charm.[8] In the same anthology, a great number of Platen's poems, but scarcely any of those I recall as favorites of my youth, not even "The Burial of Alaric." On the other hand, an endless poem on Venice—chiefly commonplace guide-book.[9] Strange how eager "critics" of the Stefan George type were to avoid anything that their forbears and predecessors had enjoyed.

21 SEPTEMBER Chapter on Giordano Bruno in Symonds's *Catholic Reaction*—excellent and renews my judgment of almost fifty years ago that these volumes contain the best their author ever did.[1] Strange that neither

[8] Joseph von Eichendorff (1788–1857). A member of the younger romantic circle and friend of Clemens Brentano and Achim von Arnim, Eichendorff was a lyric poet much influenced by German folk songs. The Stefan George selection is the three-volume anthology, *Deutsche Dichtung*, which he edited with Karl Wolfskehl in 1923.

[9] August von Platen Hallermünde (1796–1835) has been called the "German Aristophanes." In addition to his satirical plays, Platen wrote lyrical poems in which he aimed at classical purity. He was a polylinguist and a witty and biting epigrammatist.

[1] John Addington Symonds (1840–93) was a poet, biographer, essayist. Obliged to give up the law and live on the Continent for

Fulke Greville, nor Sir Philip Sidney, nor any other Englishman who saw and heard Bruno makes mention of him. Perhaps no more surprising than that neither Tocqueville nor Nassau Senior betray in letters and diaries having seen Cavour in Paris.[2] In the case of Bruno, we may still discover documents, but that Cavour should have made no impression is almost unbelievable.

22 SEPTEMBER  Whitehead in the introduction to *Adventures of Ideas* says that Gibbon wrote his *Decline and Fall* anticipating the decline of the culture of his period in favor of steam and democracy as the antique world had fallen because of barbarians and Christianity.[3] The First World War had scarcely ended when I began the intensive study of the latest centuries of antiquity, anticipating, but more consciously than Gibbon, the probable end of our world under the onslaught of material *science* at the service of power in the hands of the *proletariat*. The symptoms of decline of our culture are strangely like those of our third and fourth centuries.

---

reasons of health, he became a lover of the Renaissance; his major work, *The Renaissance in Italy*, was published in seven volumes (1875-86), two of which comprise *The Catholic Reaction*, to which B. B. here refers. Giordano Bruno (1548-1600), the subject of one of his chapters, was the Italian Dominican who was the first to state what has now become the cosmic theory. Spinoza, Leibnitz, and other later philosophers were profoundly influenced by his works. Accused of heresy, he was obliged to study and publish in Protestant countries; he taught briefly at Oxford.

[2] Cavour's visits to France in the 1850's were occasioned by his need, as the advocate of Italian independence and unity, to secure the aid of France and England against continued Austrian domination.

[3] Alfred North Whitehead (1861-1947): *Adventures of Ideas* (Cambridge, Mass., 1933). The British mathematician and philosopher was professor of philosophy at Harvard from 1924. Edward Gibbon's *History of the Decline and Fall of the Roman Empire* first appeared in six volumes over the years 1776-88.

23 SEPTEMBER Pater's *Essay on Style*.[4] Liked it much better than when it first appeared. Find it, however, too much under the influence of the then current Flaubertian ideals. Ends by saying that "great art" and "great literature" depend for their greatness on the greatness of their subject matter. Odd admission; if sincere, it should have been explained and discussed, and not put as a sort of coda to an essay, as if to make it go down with the God-fearing British reader!

24 SEPTEMBER Croce in July *Critica* on Paolo Giovio, whom, along with Ranke, he denies the title of historian; yet he fills a long article with anecdotes and portraits culled from Giovio's work.[5] Croce would Euclidize the past. I have no objection, but to him that alone is history. For me, there is nothing more effective to recall the past—and that is what I want from history—than the significant anecdote. Yet, in fact, Croce's most readable work is of the anecdotal type, and not at all Euclidean, e.g., his *Tanucci* or his *Caracciolo*, etc.

25 SEPTEMBER Pater on Wordsworth, and Matthew Arnold on the same.[6] The latter places Wordsworth on the Olympus of poets and leads him to his seat, saying

[4] *Appreciations with an Essay on Style* (1889).
[5] Paolo Giovio (1483–1552), scholarly member of the papal court (eventually bishop), wrote a history of his own times and a volume of "lives of illustrious men." Croce's article in the July, 1942, issue of *La Critica* was entitled "*La grandiosa aneddotica storia di Paolo Giovio*," and was the thirteenth in his series of "*Scrittori del primo e tardo Rinascimento*."
[6] Pater's "appreciation" of Wordsworth is included in *Appreciations with an Essay on Style*. Arnold's evaluation is contained in the Preface to his selection of the *Poems of Wordsworth* (London, 1879). Arnold's own poetry reflects his admiration for Wordsworth, whose fame had already suffered a decline by the time of his death in 1850. Arnold's edition provided the impetus for a new wave of critical and popular interest.

relatively little about his genuine merits. Pater, on the contrary, scarcely attempts to size up Wordsworth but makes us live him, feel him, enjoy the "impassioned contemplation," his master quality. Pater does not attempt to schematize, to get at the skeleton of an artist, but to present him as a work of art. Thus his criticism is in itself art—to the horror of Crocians if they knew Pater.

26 SEPTEMBER Pater followed by Matthew Arnold on Wordsworth. Arnold very appreciative, introspective, informative; leads us up to Wordsworth but does not take us in. He is like Vergil stopping short of Paradise. Pater, however, manages to unite us to the poet, to penetrate his essence, to make us live with him. He does not lay down principles, he does not schematize—at all events not first and foremost—but with a word here and a phrase there, coaxes us out of our prejudice or our mere reticence to embrace the poem.

27 SEPTEMBER In Van Wyck Brooks's *Flowering of New England,* excellent chapter on Emerson at Concord, as well as an even better one on Hawthorne in Salem. Like Pater, and perhaps even more successfully—by little biographical touches, by direct or indirect quotations, by bits of narrative—he makes us live with his subjects, enjoy their activities, and appreciate the results as if we were living them. That is criticism as art, and not merely science, and how much more effective, how much more nourishing, tonic, and entertaining.

28 SEPTEMBER Henry Michaux's *Ecuador*[7] begins too whimsically, too Dada, but of a sudden is filled with

---

[7] Paris, 1932. Michaux (born in Belgium, 1899) is a poet and painter noted for his strong personal fantasy and the exoticism resulting from his extensive travels, real and imaginary.

genuine observation and reflection, too trivial to have been jotted down by others, yet striking if only because some-one had the courage to take note of them. Of South Amer-ica, he gives the same picture as all unromantic writers—the Amazon's "prenatural" world, for by nature we mean landscape. He, Michaux, falls into chanteys the way chil-dren and peasants do, to recount to themselves the events of their day, and what they intend to do the following day, and the following.

29 SEPTEMBER Pater on Coleridge, and on Charles Lamb.[8] Not sympathizing enough with Coleridge to be interesting, and scarcely mentioning "Kubla Khan," surely the completest glimpse into what Coleridge might have done. The essay on Lamb, fascinatingly perceptive, and delicately intelligent, makes one feel Lamb, live and breathe with him, and pass days of anguish and sorrow, as well as of keen delight in rediscovering the "Old Masters" of English literature, and observing the humor not of "the town"—for which he was too humble—but of the street and of his own immediate circle.

30 SEPTEMBER Finished *Our Mutual Friend*, the first Dickens I ever succeeded in following to the end. The story fascinated me, although I disapproved of myself for this puerility, but the humor is broad, at times gross enough to be clownish (as in the dumping of Wag) and so repeti-tive. The characters are wooden, with no development, except in the case of Bella, who, by the way, strikes one as far more American than British. The narrative deliberately chopped up, so as to stuff what is essentially a short story into a huge sausage of a novel. I wonder whether *Our Mu-*

[8] Written in 1866 and 1878, respectively, both studies are included in *Appreciations with an Essay on Style.*

*tual Friend* was not written under strong influence of Eugène Sue, Hugo, and others.[9] For one thing the plot is so elaborate, and *"policier."* Then the characters! The schoolmaster with his mad jealousy based on a madder passion, leading him to murder, the egoism of his pupil, the goodness of the latter's sister, the angelic Jew, the monstrous Fledgeby, the bourgeois Podsnap, the intriguing, reciprocally hating married people, strike me as far more French than English—English for that time, at least. Am I wrong? ⁓ *"Les peuples orientaux ne professent aucun interet pour leur demeure, le climat permettant de vivre beaucoup plus en plein air que dans leur maisons. On trouve . . . le fellah, soit occupé aux travaux des champs, soit assis au café . . . les maisons ne servent qu'au repos de la nuit. . . . "* [1] I remarked this years and years ago of Italians, but later discovered it was true of all Mediterranean people. Once, at Salonica, encountered a young American missionary who hoped to cure natives of the café habit and make them good home-keeping Christians. Scipione Borghese's wife told me her father-in-law in his great palace used to sleep on a kind of shelf in one of the many sumptuous reception rooms.

[9] Sue's *Mysteries of Paris* and his *Wandering Jew* appeared in English translation some twenty years before *Our Mutual Friend* (1865). Of Victor Hugo's great novels, two had already been published in English editions: *The Hunchback of Notre Dame* (1833) and *Les Misérables* (1862).

[1] "Oriental people show no interest in their homes, as the climate allows them to live much more out of doors than in their houses. One meets . . . the fellah at his work in the fields or sitting at his café . . . his house serves only for rest at night. . . ."

## October 1942

| S | M | T | W | T | F | S |
|---|---|---|---|---|---|---|
| | | | | 1 | 2 | 3 |
| 4 | 5 | 6 | 7 | 8 | 9 | 10 |
| 11 | 12 | 13 | 14 | 15 | 16 | 17 |
| 18/25 | 19/26 | 20/27 | 21/28 | 22/29 | 23/30 | 24/31 |

1 OCTOBER Looked over last installments of Eickstedt's *Rassenkunde* [2] and scarcely find a face on the whole earth, except perhaps some ultra-African, that does not remind me of this or that acquaintance in Europe or America. Does it mean that our stock has in the course of endless time been mixed with the blood of all other races? I know of no other explanation. Nor are these rememblances confined to inferior members of our races. On the contrary. A typical instance is Clemenceau, who with all his faults was not of a lower type of mind or character.

2 OCTOBER In *Chroniques d'Égypte* for July, article on love poem of Chester Beatty Papyrus, that may

[2] Egon von Eickstedt (1892–   ): *Rassenkunde und Rassengeschichte der Menschheit* (Stuttgart, 1937). Eickstedt is an anthropologist and psychologist who has done field work in south and east Asia.

go back to the end of Eighteenth Dynasty.[3] Certainly more urbane, more refined than Song of Songs, but lacking its passion, its radiance, its directness. Is on the contrary quite flirtatious, although perhaps a thousand years earlier. There are literatures ever so much more comprehensive, more appealing to the intellect, but none so convincingly, brutally, vehemently human as the human parts of the Old Testament.

3 OCTOBER Van Wyck Brooks on Thoreau and Hawthorne and Brook Farm, too detailed, with too many overminute touches to rouse full interest. How one scents the air and feels roused and excited reading Hawthorne himself. This time Mary declaims *The Blithedale Romance*,[4] thoroughly alive but not galvanically so, as so much contemporary American story-writing. Yet his vocabulary is curiously uncertain at times, and ponderous.

4 OCTOBER Ticknor's letters of 1818 describing a twelve-day journey from Barcelona to Madrid. No wine, no food, alleviated by accidental acquaintance with Madrazo.[5] Speaks of monstrous regime and how the only decent people are in the lowest classes, and the very worst among the highest! I wonder what he would say now. He might speak better of the middle class. Strange that he says there are no fine squares, when there is one like that

---

[3] "The Chester Beatty Papyrus," in *Chroniques d'Égypte* (July, 1942). The publication is the periodic bulletin of the Fondation Reine Elisabeth, Brussels.

[4] Boston, 1852. The novel gives a picture of Brook Farm, the Transcendentalist experiment in group living, with which Hawthorne was connected for some months in the early 1840's.

[5] José de Madrazo y Agudo (1781–1859), a Spanish academic painter, was a student of J. L. David in Paris and later director of the Prado, in which some of his works now hang. Two sons and a grandson were also leading academic painters.

of the *ayuntamiento*. Did not Puerta del Sol exist yet? [6] Altogether Ticknor is an interesting observer, and given his aristocratic attitude, surprisingly liberal.

5 OCTOBER Lessing traces back a certain heroism to the gladiators of the arena who were trained not to betray any feeling under torment.[7] To rouse pity among the spectators would have soon put an end to such entertainments. "The tragedian accustomed to these spectacles could not avoid bombast and rodomontade," as exemplified by Seneca. This had not occurred to me, and proves that one does not lose time rereading the old writers even if some of their ideas are not as fresh now, nor as stimulating, as they were when first enunciated.

6 OCTOBER In Madrid, Ticknor's greatest cronies were the French ambassador, a Montmorency (whose services to his country could hardly have been as important as Ticknor believes), and Cesare Balbo. The latter is described as bursting with physical, moral, and intellectual energy. When I first came here, I read his popular history of Italy, which pleased me at the time.[8] One wonders why a young man of such promise did not realize more than he did. Was he overshadowed by his junior, Cavour? ~ Ticknor's account of the Escorial and La Granja both interesting, and the latter charming.

[6] The question is, of course, rhetorical: B. B. was familiar with the two famous Goya paintings (both in the Prado) which immortalize the popular uprising against Napoleon's troops, in 1808, with its massacre of hundreds of rebels in Madrid's central square, the Puerta del Sol, and along the Prado embankment.
[7] B. B. was reading *Heldentum der Vernunft* (Stuttgart, 1941), an anthology of selected works of Gotthold Ephraim Lessing (1729–81), the German dramatist and influential critical essayist.
[8] *Sommario della Storia d'Italia* (1846). Balbo (1789–1853) was one of the major figures in the *Risorgimento*.

7 OCTOBER Piero Fossi in his introduction on liberty in *Italiani dell'Ottocento* [9] distinguishes between liberty as freedom from foreign rule, and liberty of the individual versus the state. Does not go so far as to see that the citizen can be free only when he has all the right of a copartner or at least shareholder in the state—when he is not merely a day laborer with no voice in the running of the concern. Analyzed down to the bottom, political freedom means complete right of public discussion, and it involves the duty to keep watch and ward against abuses or incompetencies on the part of the government. More freedom than that no individual can expect in organized society.

8 OCTOBER Van Wyck Brooks's accounts of Charles Eliot Norton are probably quite exact and true, although of a Norton made younger and more active than the one I knew. That one was not too hospitable to a youth like me, although he was always courteous. Still, considering that for a couple of years I took all the courses in which he had few pupils, he might have done much more. Probably I was unattentive, and he had no desire to draw me closer. ⌒ Ran through Fabre-Luce's *Journal de la France*.[1] Beneath contempt, yet noteworthy as being the best seller among recent French publications. Hard to believe the author can be as ignorant of history as he appears to be in this book.

9 OCTOBER Glanced through Mortimer Adler's *How to Read a Book*,[2] great emphasis on the dialectical,

---

[9] Florence, 1942; based on lectures given in 1938 at the Sorbonne. The figures discussed are Rosmini, Capponi, Lambruschini, Tommaseo, Manzoni.

[1] Alfred Fabre-Luce (1899– ): *Journal de la France* (2 vols., Paris, 1942). The period covered by the volumes is May, 1939, through April, 1942.

[2] New York, 1940. Adler, former University of Chicago professor, has in the past written chiefly on Thomistic philosophy and

mathematical, and metaphysical; lip service to belles-lettres; almost no reference to history—history as written since Gibbon. ∼ Jowett's "Analysis and Introduction" to Plato's *Theaetitus* [3]—a discussion of knowledge and a criticism of the new psychology. With the last, I sympathize to the extent that I too feel its overwhelming preoccupation should be with conscious states and the fringe of these states—but touched cautiously—and that trying to get at the physiological causes will scarcely carry us forward.

10 OCTOBER Finished Van Wyck Brooks's *Flowering of New England*. Very good and informing, but wish he made much less of indirect discourses, and was more attentive to perspective. Thus I find much more told about Thoreau (and monotonously) than is really interesting, and not enough about Hawthorne, who as pure literature is worth all his other New England contemporaries put together—excepting always Emerson. The latter does not come out clearly enough personally. The author tries too hard to identify himself with his subject, and thus misses at times the proper lighting visible at the right distance.

11 OCTOBER With keenest interest, Caillaux's *Souvenirs*.[4] Talking of Dreyfus Affair, he speaks of Jews (although defending them) in terms almost of the *Protocols*

aesthetics. His major recent project has been the compiling of a "Syntopicon"—a topical guide to the basic ideas of the *Great Books of the Western World*, edited by his former Chicago colleague Robert M. Hutchins.

[3] In Volume IV of his edition of *The Dialogues of Plato*.

[4] Joseph Caillaux (1863–1944): *Ma Jeunesse orgueilleuse, 1863–1909*, Vol. I of *Mes Mémoires* (Paris, 1942). The first volume of the apologetic memoirs of a French politician whose career was punctuated by several explosive scandals.

*of the Elders of Zion.* I wish he would justify his contention, whether based on experience, on reading, or on nursery tales. I for myself have never encountered the least justification for such statements. In the synagogue one is forbidden to lift a finger toward emancipation, let alone dominion. The free-thinking Jew acts no longer as a Jew but as a European individual, even in those cases where he has other Jews like him for partners. It is never as Jews and for Jews.

12 OCTOBER Ticknor to get from Seville to Lisbon, learning that the highways are infested with robbers, joins a caravan of smugglers, whom he discovers to be jolly good fellows. Surprised to see how prosperous farmsteads and countryside looked once he got into Portugal. A little later, he is in Paris during a great political crisis in which the Duchesse de Duros is involved. There he finds one day an elderly man with his collar and his wig concealing his face, talking in authoritative but aggressive fashion. He turns out to be Talleyrand, of whom Ticknor goes on to give interesting impressions and reports of his talk—all, all, everybody as part of himself, Talleyrand, and no interest beyond.

13 OCTOBER Finished *Appreciations* and with it the rereading of Pater's entire work. It stands the past, and seems as valuable as ever for its suggestiveness, its stimulus, its specific quality of quiet, restful intellectuality. So different from the German who insists, like so many children with their toys and first watches, on smashing the subject he is treating to see how it works. So much of what I read sixty and fifty years ago, and considered first rate then, now seems old-fashioned or used up. On rereading *Gaston de Latour* nothing surprised me more than the quality of the portraits of Montaigne, Ronsard, and Bruno.

14 OCTOBER Ticknor in Vienna (1836) [5] sees Hammer-Purgstall and others, but above all Metternich, who evidently loved to talk, for he kept him an hour and a half—long after dinner was announced—explaining himself, giving expression to his disapprovals and hates and prophecies. (Few of these prophecies were later fulfilled.) Metternich hates Melbourne, particularly; he has no belief in democracy, and calls it a dissolving system, while monarchy is coagulating and creative. Ticknor considers Metternich the most distinguished person he ever met. Sees also the King of Naples, finds him unspeakably common and stupid.

15 OCTOBER Mrs. Gaskell's letters to C. E. Norton show a cultivated middle-class Englishwoman, so much like a New England woman of the same and even of the next generation.[6] Interesting about British attitude toward our Civil War—a public opinion to a certain extent due to a genuine liberalism, but considerably damped and diminished by the sense of Empire aroused by Disraeli and brought to a head by Kipling. Norton in his answers affirms and ejaculates but does not reply to the questions regarding the propriety and expedience of keeping the South in the Union by force. Touching her candid, almost animal love of Italy.

16 OCTOBER Jowett on Hegel in his Introduction to Plato's *Sophist*.[7] Singularly appreciative, and full of good

[5] The previous year, Ticknor had resigned his Harvard professorship and had returned to the Continent to collect further material for his masterpiece, *History of Spanish Literature* (1849). The extensive Spanish collection he developed went ultimately to the Boston Public Library, which he had helped to found.
[6] Elizabeth Gaskell (1810–65) wrote several novels of English village life and a biography of Charlotte Brontë; she was a contributor to Dickens's magazine *Household Words*. The correspondence has been collected in *Letters of Mrs. Gaskell and Charles Eliot Norton, 1855–65*, edited by Jane Whitehill (Oxford, 1932).
[7] In Volume IV of his edition of *The Dialogues of Plato*.

things, but "To the Hegelian all things are plain and clear, while he who is outside the charmed circle is in the mire of ignorance and logical impurity: he who is within is omniscient or at least has all the elements of knowledge under his hand." Croce and all Crocians may be characterized in the same way. Jowett speaks of all the poetical and illuminating and penetrating things, entirely irrelevant to his system, that Hegel includes in passing. I remember being struck by them when, as a young person, I tried to read Hegel.

17 OCTOBER Ticknor in Florence and Rome (1836–37), struck by the slovenliness, meanness, and cheerlessness of the private life of the most well-placed and distinguished people. Very interesting letter to [Richard Henry] Dana [Sr.] about politics and society of Europe in general, very prophetic, foresees bitter hatred growing up between the "people" and the triumphant middle classes. Amazing that a Bostonian of that time should be so unprovincial, so ready to understand Europe. I should be at a loss to name a later American so open-minded and so intelligent in all that regards "abroad."

18 OCTOBER Volume I of Caillaux's memoirs. Had greatest prejudices against him, chiefly owing to propaganda of last war. Now I have read him and am prepared to take his side, although I recall the sinister role assigned to him by Suarez in his life of Briand.[8] Am I then one of those who is always of the opinion of his last interlocutor? Perhaps it is that I can't help identifying myself with the person I am

---

[8] Caillaux, who had made no secret of his pacifist opinions throughout World War I, was charged in 1917 with "correspondence with the enemy." He spent several years in prison but re-entered the Cabinet in 1925 after recovering his citizenship through a general amnesty.

reading about, giving him sympathy and approval. Apart from all that, Caillaux knows how to present his case.

19 OCTOBER The wonderful thing about Plato is that one can read him as one reads *Gulliver* or Hans Christian Andersen, for the charm of the tone, the story; and only as one reads and rereads and reads again does the depth of the meaning reveal itself, as in Swift and Andersen—but ever and ever so much more. And how few essential problems he fails to touch that do not still worry and torment us today, and almost as many quotations as in *Hamlet*. It is a pity that the mystically allegorical side, so small a part of himself, leads to such disastrous thoughts.

20 OCTOBER Began Caillaux's *Mes Prisons*.[9] Defines patriotism as the religion of our day, and therefore as fanatical and unscrupulous. Describes the power of elaborately organized calumny, and the part Clemenceau had in it. This hero, winking at Maurras and Company [1] and taking advantage of the war and the so-called Union Sacrée, worked hard to get rid of all opposition, and thus prepared the triumphs of the Union's reactionary ideals. These are now having their day, and France can see what a day it is, and what a morning after.

21 OCTOBER Recalling how much I enjoyed his *Epic and Romance*, I have glanced through W. P. Ker's *Essays* and have been singularly disappointed.[2] Those of an

[9] Paris, 1920.
[1] Charles Maurras (1868–1952), poet and essayist, was the editor of the *Action française* and the advocate of extreme nationalism and a return to monarchy. After the liberation of France, he was sentenced to life imprisonment for his role as the chief ideologist of the Vichy collaborationist regime.
[2] William Paton Ker (1855–1923), British medievalist and professor of English literature, wrote *Epic and Romance* (1897); his *Col-*

abstract nature are puerile. Better, but not very good, are the accounts of Icelandic literature, wherein he quotes significant anecdotes with an admiration not only absurd aesthetically but adorned by his highest terms of praise, making no distinction between Scandinavians and Teutons. Not an idea in any of the articles. Of all, the best is the account of the Spanish Armada as seen by a Spaniard who served in it.

22 OCTOBER "Whether we compare the theory of Greek philosophy with the Christian religion, or the practice of the Gentile world with the practice of the Christian world, they will be found to differ more in words and less in reality than we might have supposed. The greater opposition which is sometimes made between them seems to arise chiefly out of a comparison of the ideal of the one with the practice of the other." (Jowett, *Plato* V, ccvii.) It is in this spirit that Jowett comments on Plato. Have now finished all his analyses and introductions and found them illuminating and always reasonable, as well as suggestive. Pity they are apparently as good as forgotten.

23 OCTOBER First one hundred pages of George Trevelyan's one-volume *History of England* give as intelligent an account of pre-Norman Britain as I have ever read.[3] ⁓ Began Volume II of Gomperz in French.[4] Is it because it

---

*lected Essays* were published posthumously (2 vols., London, 1925).
[3] George Macaulay Trevelyan (1876–    ): *History of England* (London, 1926). One of many historical works by the Cambridge scholar, this concise account is based on his Lowell Lectures in Boston (1924).
[4] Theodor Gomperz (1832–1912): *Les Penseurs de la Grèce: Histoire de la philosophie antique* (3 vols., Paris, 1904), translation from the German, *Griechische Denker* (1895–1902). The Austrian philologist and historian of classical philosophy taught at the University of Vienna.

is in French that I am enjoying him ever so much more than any writer in German on a philosophical subject? Perhaps so, but there is also the fact that he is as unpedantic, as clear, as evocative as the best French writers. ∼ Also began Royce's *Spirit of Modern Philosophy*,[5] which I find charmingly untechnical and humane. Admirable account of Spinoza. If only I had the leisure to read!

24 OCTOBER Finished first volume of Hawthorne's *Marble Faun*. Thus far it is a conventional tale of mystery and horror that serves to frame the notes and comments of a highly gifted stylist, who is at the same time an observant and thoughtful tourist. But an American tourist of a hundred years ago, with all his limitations as well as a compensating freshness of approach. His remarks on art are at times interesting, although not comparable with Gogol's or Balzac's.[6]

25 OCTOBER Caillaux's *Mes Prisons* confirms prejudice I always had against Barrère and in lesser degree against Charles-Roux. Nor does Ferdinando Martini come out in splendor. Interesting that neither Caillaux—so foreseeing—nor any of his interlocutors, recognized that the U.S.A. would be sure to take part if the war lasted long enough, that is, if England did not win out first.

26 OCTOBER In Ruffini's *Giovinezza di Cavour*,[7] Cavour's account of the revolution of the early 1840's in Geneva. Reveals himself as a liberal aristocrat—but an aris-

[5] Boston, 1892. Josiah Royce (1855–1916) was the Harvard philosopher who attempted to unite absolute idealism with social realism.
[6] The scene of *The Marble Faun* (1860) is Rome and the characters include American art students. Hawthorne's acquaintanceship with Europe resulted from a consular appointment he received after the election to the Presidency of his college friend Franklin Pierce, for whom he had written a campaign biography.
[7] Francesco Ruffini (1863–1934): *La Giovinezza di Cavour* (Turin, 1937). This is the work (originally written in 1916) of a liberal professor of legal history.

tocrat—the moment he sees a revolution with his own eyes. The ringleaders are *"ratés"* and their followers *"canaille."* His reading of the French Revolution should have taught him that *"ratés"* can turn into effective politicians. Not that I am out of sympathy with Cavour in this attitude of his; if I must choose a class, I'd much rather be governed by aristocrats than by proletarians. They are more likely to take comprehensive means.

27 OCTOBER Finished Caillaux's *Mes Prisons*. The hatred of him entertained by society undoubtedly due to his fiscal reforms. Their determination to keep him out of power due to fear of his carrying these reforms further. Clemenceau, who hated him for personal reasons, took full advantage of the feelings of the upper crust whose representative he had now become. Very puzzling, if Caillaux's statements are correct, is the account of him in fifth volume of Suarez's *Briand*, where Briand affirms that Caillaux was the cause in chief for the failure of a peace in 1917.

28 OCTOBER In second part of *Marble Faun*, interesting and Philistinely intelligent discussion of art. Hawthorne cannot abide most of the post-Raphael painters, and almost prefers Perugino to Raphael. His really favorite masterpieces are nevertheless Guido's "Archangel Michael of the Cappucini" and Sodoma's "Christ at the Column" (in the Pinacoteca of Siena). Very good on St. Peter's, and equally good on what the Catholic Church does for the weary and humble. Scene between Hilda and her confessor reaches rare height of beauty seldom attained by any American writer. All in all, justifies my feeling that the story serves only to link up observations of various kinds.

29 OCTOBER Kierkegaard's *Journals* (extracts in French). Astonishing outpouring of August 1, 1835, when

he was twenty-two, about himself, what he was, what God intended him to be and do—a general confession, in short. He argues the necessity of living from within and taking the shape molded and expressed by the inner life, and not modeling one's self on others. Some remarkable images, e.g.: *"Ainsi nous serait-il aisé, une fois reçu d'Ariane (l'Amour) le fil fameux, de parcourir toutes les distances du labyrinthe (la vie) et de tuer le monstre. Mais combien se lancent dans la vie (le labyrinthe) sans avoir observé cette précaution (les jeunes filles et les garçons, qu'on sacrifie chaque année au Minotaure)."* [8]

30 OCTOBER Finished Piaggia's memoirs,[9] inspired with the faith and zeal of a Columbus toward African exploration. Convinced that the savage is ferocious only when victim of evil treatment by "whites." Piaggia, like Brazza a little later, would approach them with kindness and service. He had among them the prestige of the ironworker among people still in a stone age. Has little respect for Gordon as administrator and a horror of Egyptians, whether Arab or Turk.[1] Himself direct and simple as Italians alone can be,

[8] "It should be easy, once we had received the famous thread from Ariadne (or Love), for us to find our way through all the long turns of the labyrinth (of life) and kill the monster. And yet, how many hurl themselves into life (the labyrinth) without observing this precaution ([becoming thereby] those youths and maidens who are sacrificed every year to the Minotaur)."

[9] *Le Memorie di Carlo Piaggia*, edited by G. A. Pellegrinetti (Florence, 1941). Carlo Piaggia (1827–82) was the African explorer who penetrated into unknown districts in the region around the sources of the Blue Nile.

[1] Conte Pietro Savorgnan di Brazza (1852–1905), of the next generation of Italian explorers, visited West Africa and the Congo region, beginning in 1873. He became a naturalized Frenchman and returned to Africa on behalf of the French Foreign Office, exploring and organizing territories for the French government. "Chinese" Gordon (General Charles George Gordon) was the British veteran of the Chinese rebellion of the 1860's; he came to

and his last letter, when dying alone in the heart of Africa, a touching note.

31 OCTOBER Kierkegaard asks how Christians explain the existence of so many good noble souls among the unbaptized, and gets the answer that as they are damned anyway, Satan need not take the trouble to tempt them. If that be so, then the human race after the Fall was not altogether evil, but capable of goodness, and therefore sinful only in the theological, not ethical sense, as children of Adam. Curious how Kierkegaard struggles to reconcile his Christianity with the current religiosity about him. At times his bursts of indignation remind me of Mauriac and [Georges] Bernanos. ⁓ Finished *Marble Faun*. Hawthorne ends by leaving undescribed no sight and no performance that could touch the tourist. Fascinating account of the *Carnevale*, probably far better as genre than Goethe's, which I have not reread for decades, but should expect to be more heroic. Hawthorne does not fail to do justice to the Pantheon, the Via Appia, the dome of St. Peter's, the Ghetto, etc. His art remarks very shrewd, and at times almost—but never quite—reaching the deep insight of Gogol, Balzac, or Leskov.

---

Africa in the same year as Brazza and entered the service of Ismail Pasha, the Khedive of Egypt. He became governor of the Sudan in 1877. Gordon's death in the long siege of Khartoum in 1885 was an important incident in the eventual transfer of Egypt and of the Sudan from Ottoman to British control.

```
┌─────────────────────────────────┐
│ ┌─────────────────────────────┐ │
│ │                             │ │
│ │    November 1942            │ │
│ │   ─────────────────────     │ │
│ │   S  M  T  W  T  F  S       │ │
│ │                             │ │
│ │   1  2  3  4  5  6  7        │ │
│ │   8  9  10 11 12 13 14       │ │
│ │   15 16 17 18 19 20 21       │ │
│ │  22/29 23/30 24 25 26 27 28  │ │
│ │                             │ │
│ └─────────────────────────────┘ │
└─────────────────────────────────┘
```

1 NOVEMBER Two *contes* by Hello—cases of what in New England we know, or used to know so well, as religious mania.[2] He turns them into allegorical tales of inability to believe, amounting to possession, but finally overcome by divine grace in one case; in the other it leads to the death of the victim, an opulent and pampered young woman, but it also shows the triumph of the principle through the saintliness of another young woman. Hello's Catholicism is of a very gloomy Augustinian type—in fact, of a Calvinistic kind—calculated more to frighten away, I should think, than to attract.

2 NOVEMBER Surprised how good George Trevelyan's one-volume *History of England* is. We are far from the "*Chanson de geste*" of his early years about the paladin

[2] The stories are from *Contes Extraordinaires* (1879) by Ernest Hello (1828–85), the French satirical and mystical writer.

Garibold.[3] This time there is scarcely a trace of heroics, but the rational, clear explanation of what happened—step by step across fifteen hundred years—to produce the institutions that the Englishman enjoys today. I find it informing, because some points of view are relatively new to me, and I am reminded of much that I easily forget. I get my reputation for good memory by going over the same ground often.

3 NOVEMBER Yesterday evening Igor read us a narrative sketch, so well told, with such perfect transition, that it marks him as a writer of promise, among other gifts.[4] The story is of a young girl who lost appetite, failed to take food, and finally could not be induced to eat at all. Doctors and healers tried in vain to cure her. Igor concludes that the young girl persists in her suicidal conduct because the attention of the entire village is concentrated upon her case; proud of her position, she will not relinquish it. He persuades the people to let her be, not to press her to eat, to pay no attention to her. By this and kindred means, he succeeds at last in curing her, without dominating her, without substituting his will for hers.

4 NOVEMBER In J. A. Symonds's *Catholic Reaction,* chapter on the Inquisition and all its works. Its ferocity and murderousness against individuals were known to me, but relatively new is the account of the working of the Index of

[3] The "paladin Garibold" is, of course, Giuseppe Garibaldi (1879–1950), the Italian general who fought for the British in the Boer War, for rebels in Venezuela, for the Greeks in the Balkan Wars, and for the Allies—at the head of a legion of Italian volunteers—in World War I. What B. B. characterizes as a *"chanson de geste"* —a medieval verse chronicle celebrating heroic exploits—is Trevelyan's three-volume *Garibaldi and the Making of Italy,* published nearly twenty years before the one-volume *History of England.*

[4] On Igor Markewitch, see the note for January 20.

prohibited books, making publication so difficult, so risky to everybody concerned, that printing all but stopped. Even the most highly placed men of unquestioned loyalty to the Church could not get the censors to pass their works. Besides, there was deliberate tampering with ancient texts to make them bear witness to current prejudice.

5 NOVEMBER Kierkegaard, in his diaries, speaks of being as empty as a theater after the play. He says the Irish in baptizing baby boys leave the right arm untouched by the holy water, so that it can remain pagan to brandish the sword and embrace the girls. Kierkegaard is extraordinarily full of *Einfälle*—deep, subtle, startling, suggestive, but so bound by his theology, and by Christian mysticism, that one is disgusted and halted just when one expects the most from him. Amazing, too, how little he was influenced by his German reading, although it was his chief mental food.

6 NOVEMBER Kierkegaard says that Christ came to His contemporaries and spoke to them in their own language; otherwise His mission would have failed. The implication is that if He came today He would address us in our own tongue. Suggests that Abraham, when he was about to sacrifice Isaac in despair over the goodness of God, had been suddenly seized by the fury of his pagan ancestors to slay his own son in order to propitiate his Deity. Thinks Shakespeare should not have let Lady Macbeth be unaware of her sleepwalking, thus betraying her secret, but should have made her aware of it, so that she would never dare to sleep, for fear of betraying herself.

7 NOVEMBER Symonds's *Catholic Reaction*, chapter on morals. Makes far too much of *causes célèbres*. After all, the fact that they were so carefully chronicled proves

they were rare and fascinatingly sensational events. Historians of a more popular sort are apt to forget, in their
eagerness to make themselves read, that at all times the overwhelming majority of people live relatively normal lives—
excepting of course in moments of material anarchy due to
war or pestilence. Crimes as ghastly as any of the Catholic
reaction period occur today, and percentually as many.
Who would judge our lives by them? Not we today.

8 NOVEMBER Kierkegaard oscillates between his
two preoccupations—the metaphysical-theological one and
the amorous one—always planning to write about one or
the other or both together. A charming idea is to write of a
cynic who turns dressmaker. He attracts all the rank and
fashion, and when his taste has got beyond discussion, he
begins to make for his clients clothes that render them more
and more ridiculous and vulgar. He ends by falling in love
with one of these clients, and her he wishes to dress properly. She will not have it. Kierkegaard, more than any
other Scandinavian writer, makes one regret that one cannot
read him in his own tongue.

9 NOVEMBER Finishing second volume of Gom-
perz, treating of Socrates and Plato. Clearest and most constructive account of these geniuses that I have read thus far.
Interesting that he, writing at the turn of the century,
quotes Campbell, Jowett, and Grote, while in later German
historians there is no reference to any English author except
perhaps Burnet.[5] Not the fault of the individual German, but

---

[5] Lewis Campbell (1830–1908) was professor of Greek at St.
Andrew's. In addition to his important work on Plato, he was also
the biographer of the great Plato translator, Benjamin Jowett
(1817–93). George Grote (1794–1871) was a banker who became a
self-taught historian and classicist. His twelve-volume *History of
Greece,* despite its marked bias in favor of the author's Benthamite

the arrogance of their recent attitude, ignoring either what was done elsewhere, or deliberately avoiding acknowledgments to non-Germans to whom they may be greatly indebted. This I fear will not be changed in a hurry, as the Jewish Germans, who are among the worst sinners, are sure to spread their doctrine in the countries where they have taken refuge.

10 NOVEMBER George Trevelyan on Queen Elizabeth, her sense, her political genius—so much greater than Cecil's, Walsingham's, or any other of her counselors. She certainly was the incarnation of the composite image of the overwhelming majority of all Englishmen then alive. The way George Trevelyan treads through the maze of events, characters, institutions, etc., is beyond praise. Only I wonder what a non-Anglo-Saxon would make of the book. I should like to see it commented on by Trevelyan's French vis-à-vis.

11 NOVEMBER Same Trevelyan chapter on Elizabeth's reign, explaining how the English squirearchy came about and how the English avoided castes, what was the Hebraization of the same gentry and of the middle class, as well, through intensive Bible reading, and how this led to a feeling for the language which made possible Elizabethan literature. All in all, never read more illuminating pages in any history book, and they have freed me from the prejudice I acquired against the author after reading his hagiological epic about Garibaldi and his round table.

12 NOVEMBER Reading Hello's *Contes* for the third time in forty-five years, I do not know why. They are

___
liberal sentiments, was long a standard work. The fourth of the British authorities mentioned here, John Burnet (1863–1928), was the Scottish author of several notable works on Greek philosophy.

more sermons than parables. They could have been treated with ever so much more plausibility, not to say charm, by Hawthorne. In so far as an ex-Puritan New Englander could be like a somber and querulously fanatical French Catholic, Hawthorne had a good deal in common with his contemporary Hello. Hello's stories are often allegorical, and moral-pointing, but one cannot forget the allegory, and when one becomes aware of it, this allegory adds rather than detracts, adorns and illuminates rather than desiccates the story.

13 NOVEMBER Bernard Lazare—I have been induced to peruse his *Antisémitisme.*[6] I recall his name from the Dreyfus period, but supposed he was a glib Alsatian or a Parisianized Jew of Eastern extraction. On the contrary, it turns out that he is an Israelite of ancient Avignonese origin. Besides, I suspect my friends of that time, chiefly anti-Dreyfus, may have talked disparagingly of him, and the other side failed to defend him. So, as usual when one knows nothing of a person but his name, one is too ready to pick up anything against him. However, thus far his book makes no very great impression and seems rather amateurish.

14 NOVEMBER In Ticknor, the account of the public library in Boston, to the foundation of which he contributed so much. He speaks of a M. Ruelens in Brussels who helped him. In January, 1888, I, twenty-two years old, was visiting the Royal Library of Brussels. I suppose I handed in my card. A beautiful old man came out, greeted me cordially, said he was happy to see someone from Boston because he had helped to build up its library. No doubt it was

---

[6] Published—or reissued (?)—in Paris, 1934. Lazare, who was born at Nîmes in 1866, died in 1903, three years before Dreyfus's final vindication.

147

the same M. Ruelens more than thirty years older. I feel a certain thrill to recall this tiny episode in my past. How much as a boy I owed to the Boston Public Library!

15 NOVEMBER Stephen Spender on J. M. Synge and T. S. Eliot. I entirely agree with his strictures in this and other articles of his against English speech, as well as of Van Wyck Brooks against American. But no use complaining that for the present we have no popular speech such as English may have been in the time of Shakespeare or as Irish-English seems to have remained till very lately. There is no conceivable way of going back, and it is a loss of energy and time to harp on it. Better try to find a method of vitalizing our present speech in the best way we can. It will probably come through slang, which in the U.S.A. seems to be the remedy for our plaster-cast-elementary-school-teacher English.

16 NOVEMBER Richardson's *Clarissa*, technically every bit as good as *Liaisons dangereuses*, and Clarissa's brother and sister every bit as wicked as any in latter. Miss Howe as refined and subtle in her cynicism. Richardson has the advantage over Laclos in the sense that he explains why his tale must be told by correspondence and makes the necessity plausible. I am amazed at the subtlety of the analysis into motives and characters. I wonder whether Richardson was the first to use this device of correspondence. Or did he only popularize it and make it current? [7]

[7] Whether or not he was the first to use the epistolatory device, Samuel Richardson (1689–1761) arrived at it independently. At fifty he was a successful printer; in preparing a book of sample letters for all occasions, he hit on the plan of using narrative to tie the letters together. Reversing the procedure, he went on to write *Pamela* (1740), which has been called the first modern English novel. *Clarissa* appeared in seven volumes in 1747–48. *Les Liaisons dangereuses* (1782) is the work of Pierre Choderlos de Laclos (1741–1803), the French general and novelist.

17 NOVEMBER Finished Volume I of Kierkegaard's diary. He has three themes: his relations to Regina, his relation to theology, and his relation to the public. The most haunting, for the most part, is Regina, but intellectually the most interesting are his theological dilemmas, doubts, and *cas de conscience*. His verbal felicity is extraordinary, as are his images and paradoxes. More than any other Scandinavian writer, he makes me regret that I cannot read him in his own language. I feel as if in him there must be no little that is untranslatable. Would I could get the continuation of the diary!

18 NOVEMBER Bernard Lazare's *Antisémitisme*. Depressing reading because few of the best-known Fathers and Saints of the earlier Church, and no popular preacher of later centuries down to the Reformation, escaped guilt. The worst is that even early Christian humanists like Synesius, like Cassiodorus, were not exempt. Altogether one of the most disheartening chapters of human history. One can understand that Zionists have come to the conclusion that without a territorial state Judaism will continue to suffer. Unfortunately I see no possibility of such a state.

19 NOVEMBER Finished Symonds's *Catholic Reaction*. Chapters on [Fra Paolo] Scarpi, on [Giordano] Bruno, on [Alessandro] Tassoni excellent, but his account of the Bolognese school is distressing. Symonds does not seem aware of what art is about, except as illustration, and it never seems to have entered his head that forms dictate content too powerfully to let the latter be so quickly affected by Jesuitry.

20 NOVEMBER George Trevelyan approves of the Peace of Utrecht, saying it avoided a spirit of revenge on

the part of the French. I doubt though whether the popular hatred of the English would or indeed could have been further increased unless indeed England had taken a slice of French territory. In the course of over fifty years of contact with French people, *l'esprit de revanche* I encountered was seldom because of Sédan, but rather for the loss of Alsace-Lorraine. Churchill, in his *Marlborough*, thinks that pushing the war home and bringing Louis XIV to his knees might have weakened the monarchy, led to liberalism, and forestalled the French Revolution. I wonder what Trevelyan says to that.

21 NOVEMBER Charles Andler on Burckhardt and Nietzsche, one of the most readable yet thoughtful essays on the subject.[8] The debt of the younger to the older no small one. Nietzsche was a sort of Caravaggio, a wild innovator, and no doubt the more dramatically effective writer. Yet in the long run who will appear to have understood our universe better, deeper, rounder, with a more complete sense of the whole? Surely not Nietzsche with his so limited, so explosive genius and his urge to expression— even to expressionism *modo teutonico*.

22 NOVEMBER After many years, begin to reread *Erewhon*. How plausible Butler makes it, starting out almost like *Robinson Crusoe*, and as readable as a boy's book of adventure. By the time he introduces paradoxes, he does it so gradually that you are prepared to accept them. Then comes the fun. The *cadre* has been followed by Hudson in

[8] The copy in the Berenson library is an undated Basel edition of a German translation under the title *Nietzsche und Jacob Burckhardt*. Andler (1866–1933) was a French profesor of history and political economy whose speciality was modern Germany. On the Nietzsche-Burckhardt relationship, see also the note for April 12.

his *Green Mansions* and by D. H. Lawrence in his *Woman Who Rode Away*.[9] His presentation of the hero is as the typical Englishman, as ready to play the prospector as the missionary and eager to discover the Lost Ten Tribes.

23 NOVEMBER Heine's *Romantische Schule*, after nearly sixty years.[1] How aerial, how witty, how suggestive, and at times how penetrating! One scarcely realizes one is reading German, one reads it so rapidly. Is not that the chief reason why one does not take it half so much in earnest as any ponderous German book on the same subject? Is ponderosity, then, something that impresses and inspires respect even when we carry away from it boredom and confusion? It is a question that haunts me. Few German writers are free of it, not even Goethe, nor Burckhardt, nor Nietzsche.

24 NOVEMBER Disappointed in *Erewhon* as it proceeds and becomes abstract. Not only prolix, but insistent, and its satire rather obvious to knowers of England, though probably incomprehensible to Continental people. Curious how memory eliminates and improves. I recalled only what I enjoyed and not the duller and more labored parts, which unhappily dominate in the greater part of the book. And I had hoped to be able to urge it for translation into Italian!

[9] The device of placing an Englishman (or Englishwoman) in primitive or exotic surroundings has been used in turn by these three British novelists in successive generations. Samuel Butler's utopian *Erewhon, or Over the Range* was published in 1872. *Green Mansions* (1904) was set in the lush tropics of South America by the ornithologist-novelist W. H. Hudson (1841–1922). D. H. Lawrence (1885–1930) used Mexico as the background for *The Woman Who Rode Away* (1928).

[1] Heinrich Heine (1797–1856): *Die Romantische Schule* (1835–36). Heine's attack on the "reactionary" romantic school was one of a number of satires in which the poet displayed a barbed wit.

25 NOVEMBER Carl Burckhardt's lectures.[2] The best is one on Barthélémy Micheli, a Genevese noble who will not submit to the rulings of his fellow patricians, as good as turns Catiline, takes service as military engineer in France, but ends miserably. Like Prince Rupert of the Rhine and other eminent soldiers of the time [*c.* 1675], he was a real scientist. Among the other lectures the best are on Maria Theresa and on [Friedrich von] Gentz. Surprising to find this Burckhardt bursting into enthusiasm over *Deutschtum* in a way that surely would have shocked his great kinsman Jacob.

26 NOVEMBER Finishing Gomperz's volume on Aristotle. Behind reiterated prayer and praise, he makes him out to be more of an encyclopedical intelligence than a profound or inspired one. Far from admitting it, Gomperz gives a portrait of him that reminds one of the Herbert Spencer of my younger years. The latter, too, tried to cover metaphysics, ethics, psychology, biology, and even aesthetics, but he already seems forgotten. Was he so inferior to Aristotle, or is it only that the Greek of the fourth century B.C. had the advantage of being the first in the field?

27 NOVEMBER Ticknor home in Boston, seeing Civil War approaching, hoping against hope it may be avoided or deferred, but not surprised when it bursts out. All through his life, he seems to have had extraordinary good sense for politics, both at home and abroad, although his point of view is on the whole as conservative as possible for a man with such a faith in the political sense of the Ameri-

[2] *Gestalten und Mächte: Reden und Aufsätze* (Zürich, 1941). The historian and diplomat (born in Switzerland in 1891) has been professor of modern history at both Zürich and Geneva and has served as president of the International Red Cross.

cans of his day. What would he say today? Yet the truly dangerous elements today are the descendants not of later immigrants but of the very people he trusted so well.

28 NOVEMBER Madariaga's *Anarchie ou Hierarchie.*[3] Seldom read anything on politics that goes so thoroughly over the ground of my own thinking on the subject, till toward the end he comes to the methods of carrying on the modern community. Not that I disagree, but his suggestions are too new and at the same time too definite for me to take up immediately, although some have occurred to me repeatedly in the course of the years. At all events, a most penetrating and stimulating little book—one that I ought to have read when it appeared in 1936.

29 NOVEMBER Gomperz's *Greek Thinkers,* Volume III, ends with a most appreciative account of Theophrastus. I should venture to guess that Theophrastus is more attractive to Gomperz than Aristotle himself. Some pages about Straton of Lampsacus, whom he reports as saying that without thought no sensation is possible—a conclusion to which my own thinking has brought me, independently of all philosophies, just trying to suck out the essence of my reflection on my own experience. It is heartening to come across fellow adventurers who have made the identical discoveries.

30 NOVEMBER Finishing Ticknor. Pity such an observer, and with such statesmanlike insight into the bearing

[3] Paris, 1941, translated by the author himself from the original English edition of 1936. Salvador de Madariaga (1886–    ) is the Spanish philosopher, historian, and scholar of literature who was a League of Nations official for many years and then professor of Spanish literature at Oxford until he became the Spanish Republic's ambassador to Britain and then to France.

of events, has left so little about our Civil War, and nothing at all about Reconstruction. Would gather that he was not too favorable to Lincoln and his way of conducting affairs. Shall we Anglo-Saxons do better after this war if we win it? I have great fears we shall muddle and sin, not so much out of wickedness as out of crass ignorance. Save us, Good Lord! ⁓ Maritain's *Confession de Foi,* published recently in New York.[4] Agree heartily with his purely human-political values, but dislike a certain pharisaical arrogance that seems inseparable from those who are so sure that they possess the truth. As for going back to St. Thomas and finding all one needs to know there about ultimates, *il se contente de peu—* or he is like those painters who want to go back to tempera, hoping to find there the inspiration and technique that will allow them to display their genius. ⁓ Opening chapters of Raïssa Maritain's *Grandes Amitiés.*[5] Touching account of her childhood in South Russia. In many respects parallel to my childhood in Lithuania. She tells of leaving Russia at ten, as I did, and of the strange new world she encounters, and of her zest for knowledge, and of taking it as a matter of course that she is to get the best education to be had. Less charming, although no less interesting, are her contacts with Bergson and his philosophy, as well as her companionship and marriage with Maritain.

---

[4] Jacques Maritain (1882–    ): *Confession de Foi* (New York, 1941). This short work had first appeared, in English, in *I Believe* (edited by Clifton Fadiman, 1939). The French philosopher has written on aesthetics, ethics, and politics, in addition to metaphysics. Originally influenced by Henri Bergson and his philosophy of "creative evolution," he became a follower of St. Thomas Aquinas.
[5] Raïssa Urmansov Maritain (1883–    ): *Les grandes amitiés* (New York, 1941). Mme Maritain, a poetess of Russian-Jewish origin, was a fellow-student of Jacques Maritain at the Sorbonne. Both were converted to Catholicism in the year following their marriage (1905).

## December 1942

| S | M | T | W | T | F | S |
|---|---|---|---|---|---|---|
| | | 1 | 2 | 3 | 4 | 5 |
| 6 | 7 | 8 | 9 | 10 | 11 | 12 |
| 13 | 14 | 15 | 16 | 17 | 18 | 19 |
| 20/27 | 21/28 | 22/29 | 23/30 | 24/31 | 25 | 26 |

1 DECEMBER In Raïssa Maritain's *Les grandes amitiés,* her account of Bergson and his intuitionalism as opening the way which led to her conversion to Catholicism, through the example and influence of Léon Bloy. She gives a photo of him, and it might be one of the most ferociously disagreeable of French *douaniers.*[6] I have always instinctively dreaded mysticism (although fascinated by it) as endangering the light of reason—a poor light, nearly always smoking, and often stinking, but yet all we have to let us go forward a few feet in a century toward a positive, materially better world, opening out greater possibilities of genuine and not merely ecstatically illusive states of euphoria.

2 DECEMBER Volume I of Gomperz—never read such a clear account of both Pythagoreanism and Orphism.

[6] Léon Marie Bloy (1846–1917), French Catholic novelist and essayist, was a passionate and vigorous writer and a man of violent temperament.

155

The latter a middle-class revolt against oligarchy, as well as transfer of hope to a life beyond the grave. In this connection, Gomperz quotes an Egyptian confession of sins followed by a list of good deeds, implying a humanitarianism surpassing anything I can recall in Old or New Testament or in Jesuits or Christian Fathers. But what does not seem clear is the precise date of this confession and apology.

3 DECEMBER Finished George Trevelyan's one-volume *History of England*. Never read anything so satisfactory on similar subject in such small compass. It is a serious and successful attempt to explain what has made the England of today, going from significant joint to significant joint, appreciating it both for its own value and as a link in the chain, ignoring superfluities, never sinking to anecdote. Free, too, from undue self-congratulation, with no touch of nationalism. In short, as good a history of one's own country as human nature at its best will achieve.

4 DECEMBER Gomperz on pre-Socratics, as delightful as the later volume. I admire his insistence on the proposition that errors of geniuses are so much more creative than the invincible but blind-alley conclusions of correct thinking. The conclusions of the last are too often tombstones, while those of the others are more like resurrections or gestations leading to new births. I enjoy particularly Gomperz's account of Xenophon, Zeno, Parmenides, and Empedocles.

5 DECEMBER Butler's *Erewhon Revisited*, much better than *Erewhon*.[7] Yet faulty as compared with great satire like Swift's *Gulliver*, which combines satire and story

[7] The sequel appeared in 1901, nearly thirty years after the publication of *Erewhon*.

so that they are indistinguishable, and which a child can read without becoming aware of the satire. In Butler, the story is often good indeed—and Iram is a creation—but the satire remains abstract and outside the tale, and consequently gets prolix and prosy. The moment satire is naked it should be epigrammatic and never expository, nor even explanatory.

6 DECEMBER  Here and there in Lessing. How refreshingly sensible he is, how sturdily reasonable—almost Johnsonian—but with a much wider intellectual horizon. He makes pity the important element in tragedy, but the German word *"Mitleid"* is a translation of "sympathy." Pity is the easiest way to sympathy, and sympathy soon leads to life-enhancing identification, if that is what the poet wishes to procure for us, so that we live, suffer, and exalt with his hero.

7 DECEMBER  Finished Royce's *Spirit of Modern Philosophy.* Pretty interpretation of the great thinkers from Kant to Schopenhauer, but when he comes to his own Cosmos, I lacked the patience to follow it with sufficient attention to do justice to it. On the other hand, the fact that I could not persuade myself that it was worth while to follow him closely is in itself for my age and experience a kind of judgment. Royce was a younger contemporary of Browning with his "somehow good"—not on a human plane alone (where I would gladly accompany him), but beyond.

8 DECEMBER  *Opinions of Oliver Allston,* a clever device of Van Wyck Brooks for putting out stray notes.[8] Delighted with his orthodoxy in matters of literature and

---

[8] *Opinions of Oliver Allston: On Literature Today* (New York and London, 1941).

life. Chuckled over his attacks on that solemn humbug of T. S. Eliot, his criticism of Henry James, his definitions of American states of mind, his courage in telling his countrymen what he thinks of them. The fact that his books sell proves there is a large public that is not offended by his plain speaking and his unflattering analyses.

9 DECEMBER William James's "The Energies of Men," [9] in which he urges that people do not know what they are capable of till they have tried. I agree entirely about a new wind and another and another, but in my own experience, after working at maximum for a couple of years when I was forty, I had a serious breakdown from which it took me as long to recover. Since then every strain has led to fits of melancholies, some of a very distressing kind. Now I do not dare to go on when I feel fatigue approaching, and make a point of stopping in time.

10 DECEMBER "A Place of One's Own" and "Open the Door!"—stories by Osbert Sitwell, surprisingly well written and aware.[1] He seldom gets away from the smart set, but remains detached and not absorbed by it as is Sylvia Thompson or even Violet Trefusis—inexcusable in the latter, who was brought up in a society above it. Sitwell's irony is delicate and human, never bitter or roughshod. He knows

[9] In *Memories and Studies* (London and New York, 1911), edited by his son. James, originally a physician, taught at the Harvard Medical School until 1880, and thereafter at the University's department of psychology and philosophy, where the young B. B. first came to know him.

[1] Both stories were published in London in 1941—the former by itself and the latter in a collection, also called *Open the Door!* Sir Osbert (1892–    ) was a member of the Bloomsbury circle; he is a poet and novelist and the author of several volumes dealing with the history of his remarkable family.

his English lower and even middle classes, the latter a real feat.

**11 DECEMBER** Guy Pearce Jones's *Two Survived*,[2] story of a boatload who got away from the sinking of their ship and were at sea some twenty days. Only two survived when the boat drifted to the Bahamas. There they were well treated and brought back to health, whereupon one of them shipped from New York to return to England on a vessel that was torpedoed, with all drowned. Account of sufferings from hunger and thirst is vividly but unsensationally told. Most of the boatload died of wounds inflicted when torpedoed or by jumping overboard to avoid unendurable tortures of hunger and thirst. Compares with *Moby Dick*.

**12 DECEMBER** Finished Gomperz. Cannot recall reading a work on a similar subject that I enjoyed as much. He is accused of being too much of an empiricist and favoring his *coreligionnaires* in ancient Greece. He certainly writes of Democritus and Thucydides with a warmth and zest far beyond what he attributes to Aristotle or even Plato. The last he regards as the greatest, or at least as one of the greatest, writers that ever lived rather than as the greatest of philosophers. There I venture privately to agree with him on my own experience.

**13 DECEMBER** Aristotle's *Metaphysics*,[3] Book III, reads like so much of Lewis Carroll, and at times even like Gertrude Stein. By the way, what an influence this proto-Semite is having. ∼ A long story by Elizabeth Bowen, "The

---

[2] New York, 1941.
[3] The edition in B. B.'s library was the Loeb Classical Library (2 vols.).

Disinherited," [4] has page upon page of a confession couched in a lingo largely Steinese. Indeed it is difficult nowadays to read any belles-lettres in the English tongue that is not tarred with that so-smudging brush!

14 DECEMBER William James's *Pluralistic Universe* [5] —do not recall reading it before. Perfect joy to encounter such clear statement and such bold courage in pricking bubbles. Splendid how he shows up Hegel and other lawgivers, pointing out that their systems are based on wishful thinking and that they defend them with a dialectic that serves only to trouble the waters of thought so that they may fish out of it a justification of their temperamental theories. Informing and interesting chapter on Fechner.

15 DECEMBER A. E. Taylor's "People's Booklet" on Aristotle. [6] I wonder how many of the "lower orders" for whom it is intended can follow it. There is no condescension to popular lack of preparation for tackling such a subject. It is very informative, no doubt, but dry as a bone, and at times pretty technical. For me the chief interest lay in references to the Schoolmen and Dante in their relations to Aristotle. I wish Taylor wrote more explicitly on these relations, with which he evidently is well acquainted.

16 DECEMBER Reading and enjoying definitions in Book XI and XII of Aristotle's *Metaphysics*. Amazing that in the fourth century B.C. definition should already have been so precise, clear, yet so subtle—and more still that the

[4] This story by Miss Bowen (born 1899), the Anglo-Irish novelist of British upper-class life, appears in *Look at All Those Roses* (London, 1941).
[5] London, 1909. Based on his Hibbert Lectures at Manchester College.
[6] Published in 1912 as No. 67 in "The People's Book" series.

subjects for definition should have been selected with such a remarkable sense of what was significant enough to be worth defining. Who else thought of such a thing outside the Greek world? The Hindus surely not. I suspect when they later did so it was under Greek influence.

17 DECEMBER Finished Elizabeth Bowen's *Look at All Those Roses*, a series of stories, wonderfully written with evocative and penetrating epithets, and with a rhythm of her own, but of a dreariness surpassing Chekhov's, and ever so much more self-consciously decadent. It is the picture of a level of society between the humble gentry and the intelligentsia, not knowing what to live for or even how to make a living. Happily it comprises but a very small percentage of British people, even if a conspicuous one, far too conspicuous, as is the case in America with its Faulkners, and Hemingways, and their exaggerating followers.

18 DECEMBER Read far into Scott's *Waverley*,[7] but it has not yet got alive. Interesting description of landscape, condition, and state of mind in Scotland, but characters are thus far defined rather than created. How account for its instantaneous popularity when it appeared? Perhaps people were tired of vague horrors, wonders, and mystery, and rather enjoyed almost matter-of-fact information—particularly as it was of those Celtic Highlands for which the reading of Ossian had well prepared the public.[8] The scene is now set, and we shall see whether Scott can already make things happen.

[7] Sir Walter Scott (1771–1832): *Waverley, or 'Tis Sixty Years Since*. Scott's first novel, originally published in 1814, was set in Scotland of the middle eighteenth century.
[8] Barely twenty years had passed since the death of James Macpherson, whose purported translations of the poems of the Gaelic bard Ossian had been widely read and had provoked continuing controversy over the question of their authenticity.

19 DECEMBER In P. E. More's *Hellenistic Philosophers*,[9] the chapters on Plotinus and Diogenes—excellent. Around these, and Epictetus as well, More manages to give an interesting account of the spiritual condition of the ancient world in the second, third, and fourth centuries of our era. He does not flatter the achievements of Christianity, but he does not go on to blame the theologians enough for wasting the best energies of the time on vain disputes—indeed, he must value them, seeing the way he writes of Athanasius and other monsters of power-lust.

20 DECEMBER Finished William James's *Pluralistic Universe*. Enjoy his attack on Rationalism, Conceptualism, etc., particularly of the Hegelian species. But cannot revel as he does in the welter of *things*, which is either ecstasy, anarchy, or bedlam. Concepts, as William James knows well, are indispensable instruments, but in his distaste for backing them as ends and not merely means, he wants to get rid of them altogether. It is worse than getting rid of all receptacles for ladling up liquids.

21 DECEMBER In More's *Hellenistic Philosophers*, the chapter on skeptics, very interesting on Sextus Empiricus, whom More describes as a philosopher who advocated, not nihilistic skepticism, but open-mindedness. How does this differ from the agnosticism with regard to ultimates that has marked so many members of the last few generations—an attitude of which I suspect More would not approve at all? I wonder why I go on reading philosophy. I seldom get to the heart of it. Yet curiosity drives me forward.

[9] Princeton, 1923. Paul Elmer More (1864–1937) was editor of *The Nation* and then a professor at Princeton. He was an associate of Irving Babbitt in the humanistic movement and an authoritative writer on the Greek philosophers.

**22 DECEMBER** Steinbeck's *Of Mice and Men*,[1] artistically fine, but that can scarcely account for its popularity. Is it not its symbolical, allegorical overtones? Lennie represents sheer strength and force, power used with no evil intention, but with no self-knowledge either, nor even sense of any kind. Indeed his best intentions are the worst in effect. George is the liberal who is attached to the state, and yet feels at long last that he must destroy it lest it blunderingly destroy everything else. The other figures are very good rubble or even ashlar. In some ways, as sheer art, Steinbeck reminds me of Verga.[2]

**23 DECEMBER** Happened to fall on Britannica article on Aristotle by Thomas Case—a name new to me.[3] By far the best account of "the Stagirite," admirable philologically, and as clear as possible on cosmology, rhetorics, physics, and all his other encyclopedic pursuits. Surprisingly better than A. E. Taylor's booklet. Leaves one, however, curiously uncertain to what extent one has the very words of Aristotle—although his teaching we certainly have. I only wish Case had added a word or two about Aristotle *à travers les âges.*

**24 DECEMBER** Reading Steinbeck and Caldwell, it occurred to me to look into *This Generation*, an anthology of English and (chiefly) American prose and verse since 1914, to see what of theirs it contained. They are not even mentioned, which means that their reputations had not yet

[1] John Steinbeck (1902–    ): *Of Mice and Men* (New York, 1937).
[2] Giovanni Verga (1840–1922) was an Italian novelist and short-story writer much concerned with the poverty and struggles of the Sicilian peasants. His simple style and strict attention to accuracy has earned his art the name *"verismo."* D. H. Lawrence translated some of his works into English.
[3] Case (1844–1925), a pupil of Jowett, was for many years professor of moral and metaphysical philosophy at Oxford.

163

reached the editors of that publication.[4] Yet they had already published enough to compare with others inserted. Thomas Wolfe is mentioned but nothing of his is given. Strange medley, significant of what, representing what?

25 DECEMBER Books XIII and XIV of Aristotle's *Metaphysics*, chiefly a labored and overelaborate effort to combat the notion that numbers have a substantial existence apart from the things they enumerate. All this evidently absorbed the best minds of the fourth and third centuries B.C., yet how otiose it all is to a mind like mine—as indeed so much that passionately preoccupied theologians and pseudo scientists in the following centuries, down to our own time. Are superior minds so in love with their own functioning that they care not what they function about?

26 DECEMBER Erskine Caldwell's story translated by Elio Vittorini. About dice-players, a tale of beastly violence on the one hand and mere cowardice on the other. Why has Elio Vittorini chosen to translate this out of all Caldwell's stories? Is it that he feels fascinated by bestiality and violence, and the abject spectacle of cowardly submission? One is tempted to think so, seeing the stories he has chosen to translate for an anthology of American stories he and others have made. Still unpublished for political reasons.[5]

27 DECEMBER Heine's *Deutschland*, remarkably free from clownish wittiness in contrast to his *Romantische*

[4] *This Generation: A Selection of British and American Literature from 1914 to the Present* (Chicago, 1939) was edited by Eda Lou Walton and George K. Anderson.
[5] The anthology was later published in Milan as *Americana*, with Vittorini listed as its editor. (On Vittorini, see the note for February 12.) The Caldwell story is "*Il Mondo ai Dadi.*"

*Schule,* which has too much of it.[6] Of course he avoids telling what the philosophers were thinking about, but he gives a good account of their influence and its consequences. His observations and comments on England are very good, suggestive and penetrating.[7] As a prophet foretelling the future he is extraordinary. What he foretells about Germany when Thor and Wotan and their followers come to life again, we are living now—all of us, not only the French whom he warns.

28 DECEMBER *Oeconomia,* ascribed to Aristotle, in the Loeb Classics. First book delightful. The second, a series of anecdotes chiefly concerned with the tricks of "sovereigns"—whether imperial, royal, municipal, legitimate, or usurpers—in raising taxes and contributions from reluctant subjects. Some of it amusing enough, but not always bearing on what the first book had to say.

29 DECEMBER Third book of *Oeconomia,* attributed to Aristotle. Until triumph of "Woman's Movement," which has influenced us all, it would have been regarded as presenting a high, almost unattainable ideal of the marital relations—insisting, as it does so much, on the deep respect that must enter into real love. On the whole, it seems higher than any other ideal ever expressed, superior to Jewish or Christian. The more I read Greek philosophy and thought, the less do I understand what good Christianity has tried to actuate that Greece did not invent.

---

[6] Heine's castigation of his native country appears in three parts: *Deutschland I* (1834), *Deutschland II* (1853-54), and *Brief über Deutschland* (published posthumously, 1859). They are reprinted in Volumes III and IV of his *Gesammelte Werke* (12 vols., Hamburg, 1876).

[7] *England* (1828) also appears in the 1876 edition of the *Gesammelte Werke,* Volume II.

30 DECEMBER Seignobos's *Histoire Sincère de la Nation Française*,[8] free from chauvinism and even from class feeling but too dry, too chronicle-like. Instructive as manual, but not readable. Best naturally in describing institutions, culture, and progress—the last almost with eloquence. Military events he ignores, and gives almost no space to Napoleon and none to his campaigns. Yet a little panache, a touch of epic, cannot and should not be avoided in writing history.

31 DECEMBER Steinbeck's *Battle* in Italian translation, as I cannot lay hold on the original.[9] Very taking and impressive, but scarcely more than a splendid piece of propaganda, as well done as the genre permits. No room for full development of characters, for the protagonist is not a person but an event. The event itself is somehow not shapely enough in treatment, nor sufficiently exciting. One is tempted to guess the author did not know whether to give importance to the persons or the happenings. Admirable things said, by the way. ∼ Heine's notes on England. Intelligent at times, and witty, but with no general understanding, and no sympathy whatever. Quite the contrary. Whence this antipathy to the English on the part of almost all Continentals, except the few like Tocqueville or the young Cavour, who took an intellectual interest in real politics? The others were and are still victims of the propaganda forged by the Vatican and Spain against Queen Elizabeth.

[8] Paris, 1933. Charles Seignobos (1854–1942), who taught at the University of Paris, wrote many books on French history and civilization, some of which have been widely used as textbooks.
[9] *In Dubious Battle* (1936), Steinbeck's novel of the problems of migrant fruit-pickers in California and of their organization into labor unions during the Great Depression, appeared in an Italian translation, *La Battaglia* (Milan, 1940), by Eugenio Montale (1896–    ), an Italian poet and critic.

# Index of Persons

Authors and other individuals discussed or alluded to in the Diary are included in this INDEX OF PERSONS. Books, essays, short stories, and periodicals are included in a separate alphabetical INDEX OF TITLES, beginning on page viii.

Many of the persons or works to which B. B. has made allusion are identified in the footnotes, which also include certain supplementary data as well. Persons and titles in this latter category have been omitted from both Indexes in order that these lists may reflect only B. B.'s actual reading and Diary comments during the year 1942.

i

Petrarch, 16
Phaedo, 26
Phidias, 104
Piaggia, Carlo, 140–1
Pindar, 77
Pinder, Wilhelm, 114
Pirenne, Henri, 6, 9, 11, 14
Pizzetti, Ildebrando, 5
Platen (Hallermunde), August von, 122
Plato, 21–8, 30, 35, 40–2, 44, 48, 55–83 *passim*, 89–104 *passim*, 109, 110, 114, 116, 118, 132, 134, 136, 137, 145, 159
Plotinus, 36, 162
Poe, Edgar Allen, 76
Poggio Gherardo, 39
Poincaré, Raymond, 6, 73
Polybius, 54
Praz, Mario, 108, 109–10
Prescott, William H., 121
Protagoras, 64
Pushkin, Aleksandr Sergeyevich, 76
Pythius, 5

Ramses the Great, 34
Ranke, Leopold von, 3, 5, 7, 23 *n.*, 124
Raphael Sanzio, 37, 46, 78, 139
Reininger, Robert, 112
Rembrandt, 12
Renan, Ernest, 106
Ricciotti, Giuseppe, 106
Richardson, Samuel, 148
Ricketts, Charles, 107–8
Rilke, Rainer Maria, 79
Rio, Alexis François, 118
Rivière, Jacques, 12
Robertson, John Mackinnon, 55, 56
Ronsard, Pierre de, 120, 133
Rosé (Briand interpreter), 6
Rosset, François de, 53 *n.*
Rossetti, Dante Gabriel, 105
Rostoptchine, Count Feodor, 42, 43, 45
Rousseau, Jean-Jacques, 35 *n.*, 97

Royce, Josiah, 138, 157
Ruelens, M. (Royal Librarian of Brussels), 147–8
Ruffini, Francesco, 138
Rupert, Prince (of the Rhine), 152
Ruskin, John, 7, 8, 9, 12, 21, 27–9, 36–8, 40 *n.*, 43, 86–7

St. John, Henry (Lord Bolingbroke), 92
Sainte-Beuve, Charles Augustin de, 64, 65 *n.*, 66, 69, 70
Sallust, 54
Salutati, Coluccio, 20
Santoli, Vittorio, 86
Scarpi, Fra Paolo, 149
Schelling, Caroline. *See* Caroline
Schelling, Friedrich Wilhelm von, 35, 38 *n.*, 39, 40 *n.*, 43, 45, 54, 76, 79
Schiller, Friedrich, 28, 30, 32–3, 35, 44, 51 *n.*, 55, 121 *n.*
Schlegel, August Wilhelm von, 35, 36, 40–1, 47, 54, 55, 73, 76, 117 *n.*, 118
Schlegel, Caroline. *See* Caroline
Schlegel, Friedrich von, 35, 36, 37 *n.*, 47, 55, 76, 83–4, 86, 90–1, 93, 102, 118, 121 *n.*
Schleiermacher, Friedrich Daniel Ernst, 40, 76 *n.*, 84
Schopenhauer, Arthur, 157
Schorn, W., 28 *n.*
Schumann, Robert, 5
Scott, Sir Walter, 161
Ségur, Comte A. de, 42–3, 45
Seignobos, Charles, 166
Seneca, 109, 130
Senior, Nassau, 123
Sextus Empiricus, 162
Shakespeare, William, 8, 12, 51 *n.*, 72 *n.*, 76 *n.*, 86, 136, 144, 148
Shaw, George Bernard, 52
Shelley, Percy Bysshe, 32, 33, 92, 95, 104
Shirer, William L., 8, 9, 11

# Index of Persons

vii

## Index of Titles

[See note at the head of the INDEX OF PERSONS, on page i.]

# Index of Titles

ix

# Index of Titles

# Index of Titles

xiii

### A NOTE ABOUT THE AUTHOR

BERNARD BERENSON, born in Lithuania in 1865, was, as a child of ten, taken to Boston by his parents and remained there till his graduation from Harvard in 1887, when he made his first journey to Italy. Although he made frequent trips back to the United States, he lived from 1900 on in his famous villa, I Tatti, at Settignano, near Florence. Here he brought together his own fine collection of paintings and an extraordinary library. His rise to a position of pre-eminence in the field of art history began in 1894 with the publication of the first of his many books on Italian art, which have become classics in their field. Of these *The Italian Painters of the Renaissance* is perhaps the best known. As an art expert he advised dealers and collectors alike, exerting an unparalleled influence in the formation of the art collections that are the basis of America's great public and private museums. As a scholar, molder of taste, philosopher, writer of letters, and conversationalist Bernard Berenson occupied for more than half a century a unique place in the world of art and letters. His magnificent assemblage of books, some forty thousand volumes carefully chosen over the decades, remains his ultimate monument. This great collection, one of the world's finest private libraries, he bequeathed—along with I Tatti itself and its art treasures—to Harvard University. He died in October 1959.

## A NOTE ON THE TYPE

THE TEXT of this book was set on the Linotype in
Janson, a recutting made direct from the type cast
from matrices long thought to have been made by
Anton Janson, a Dutchman who was a practicing
type-founder in Leipzig during the years 1668–87.
However, it has been conclusively demonstrated that
these types are actually the work of Nicholas Kis
(1650–1702), a Hungarian who learned his trade
most probably from the master Dutch type-founder
Dirk Voskens.

The type is an excellent example of the influential and sturdy Dutch types that prevailed in England prior to the development by William Caslon
(1692–1766) of his own incomparable designs, which
he evolved from these Dutch faces. The Dutch in
their turn had been influenced by Claude Garamond (1510–1561) in France. The general tone of
the Janson, however, is darker than Garamond and
has a sturdiness and substance quite different from
its predecessors. This book was composed, printed,
and bound by Kingsport Press, Inc., Kingsport,
Tennessee. The paper was manufactured by S. D.
Warren Company, Boston. Typography and bind-
ing design by WARREN CHAPPELL.